HIPPERHOLME AND LIGHTCLIFFE

MEMORIAL STRAY

R.A.S.C.
VERBROEDERING
1016 Cⁱᵉ
BELGIUM

THIS MEMORIAL
WAS ERECTED AND
THE STRAY
DEDICATED TO THE
PUBLIC FOREVER
IN REMEMBRANCE OF
THOSE RESIDENTS WHO
GAVE THEIR LIVES AND
IN GRATITUDE TO
THOSE SURVIVORS WHO
GAVE THEIR SERVICES
IN THE EUROPEAN WAR
1914 - 1918

IN HONOUR OF
THOSE WHO GAVE
THEIR LIVES IN
THE SERVICE OF
THEIR COUNTRY
IN THE 2nd WORLD WAR
1939-1945

HIPPERHOLME AND LIGHTCLIFFE

MEMORIAL STRAY

Bob Horne

Lightcliffe and District Local History Society

FESTINA LENTE

Published 2023 by Lightcliffe and District Local History Society
www.lightcliffehistory.org.uk

ISBN 978-1-9162983-4-7

Designed and Typeset in Adobe Garamond by Malcolm Heron

Printed by Amadeus Press, Ezra House, West 26 Business Park,
Cleckheaton, West Yorkshire, BD19 4TQ.

www.amadeuspress.co.uk

Also published by Lightcliffe & District Local History Society.

Village Voices (2007), compiled by Bob Horne & John Brooke.

Educating the Generations (2020), John Brooke.

In the Shadow of Lightcliffe's Old Tower: Two Churches and a Churchyard (2022),
Dorothy Barker & Ian Philp.

Walterclough Valley: A History (2022), John Wharton.

Drawn on the Landscape (2023), Alan Greenwood.

Foreword

Sometime before Covid – I think probably after one of the Lightcliffe History Society meetings – Bob and I were chatting. He said it was the centenary of the Stray in 2023, and we should write a book about it. What! I thought. There must be all of a couple of pages to describe how it came to be. I promptly forgot about it.

However, Bob would bring up this idea occasionally and I realised he was serious about the project. After all he has published several books, and knows how to set about such a task. At this point I let him know that if he wanted to go ahead, I would be happy to help and maybe provide a few photos.

Then Covid struck, the history society meetings ceased for two years, and nothing much was mentioned until the autumn of 2022 . After the first society meeting in late September Bob suggested that a few of us could meet at the Lightcliffe Tea Rooms to discuss how to research the proposed book. In the event four of us were there: Ian Philp, an authority on local history and a guide on Heritage Walks, Bob's wife Claire, Bob, and me.

I won't elaborate on our investigations, which entailed several sessions at the Brighouse and Halifax libraries during the following months. Bob also met with others to flesh out the story. During the compiling of the wealth of information gathered, Bob's laptop struggled to do an efficient job, so he invested in a more powerful computer enabling him to format the book when it was ready to be printed.

Bob and I grew up a few doors away from each other, with the Stray across the road. From the early 1950s it was our playground and sportsground. It was a mere thirty years old at the time, and it is gratifying to know that it still attracts the young people of the village to its wide acres.

I'm sure you will agree after reading this illuminating story of the history of the fields which became the Memorial Stray, the unveiling of the memorial and the opening of the surrounding parkland, and some of the later developments, that it will remain an important historical account for future generations of Hipperholme and Lightcliffe residents.

Dave Lister

25 May 2023

Preface

I have lived close to the Stray for more than seventy years. It is where the Hipperholme and Lightcliffe children and young teenagers of my generation gathered. For me it holds memories of endless games of cricket during summer holidays, football and sledging in the winters, games of hide and seek and its variants – Kick t' Can and 'Oppit, Twenty-fivers, 'I draw a snake on this man's back …' – the swings, the slide, monkey climb and other playground equipment. I assumed it had always been there. But, as Dave Lister says in his foreword, it was only thirty years old when we first knew it.

The fields, latterly known after its landowners as Smithson Park, were bought by public subscription and handed over to Hipperholme Urban District Council in 1923. We are coming up to its centenary and it was that thought, a few years ago, which prompted me to consider researching its origins and the early years of its history with a view to writing what might have been a booklet. In the event, the abundance of material has resulted in a publication of much greater length.

My starting point has been 1820. I have looked at certain significant events of the following hundred years: the Crow Nest Sale of 1867, transfer of ownership within the Smithson family, and the auction of 1907, when the whole area might have been sold for housing. The Stray was the final commemoration in our area of the lives of the villagers who had died during the First World War, and I have given accounts of other memorials unveiled at the time in Hipperholme, Lightcliffe, Bailiff Bridge, Norwood Green and Coley. Finally, council minutes and newspapers have painted a thorough picture of the care taken in the upkeep of this wonderful playing field. My history ends with the Silver Jubilee Gala of 1977, fifty-four years after the opening ceremony of 9 September 1923.

Our village would be a very different place without the Stray. I walk across it on most days and it is almost always busy with people of all ages. Researching and writing this book, recalling my early years and those who shared its freedoms in the 1950s and early 1960s, has been such an enjoyable project. I hope I have conveyed some of that enjoyment in the pages that follow.

Bob Horne

17 June 2023

Acknowledgements

A number of people have been of invaluable help during the writing of this book. I mention them in no particular order.

Peter Bottomley has refined old photographs, some of them faded images from newspapers, taken with an iPhone from microfiche copies at the central library. He has also adapted maps, designed the cover and generally been a sound source of advice over coffee in the Lightcliffe Tea Rooms. Dorothy Barker, secretary of the Friends of St. Matthew's Churchyard, researched details of those remembered at our local churches. The names of these young soldiers, and one woman, are contained in Appendix 1. My wife, Claire Horne, and I, along with Dave Lister and Ian Philp, were the team who set out in December 2022 to look through the minutes of the Hipperholme Urban District and Brighouse Town Councils. These had been kindly transferred from Halifax to Brighouse library, where a room was set aside for us to study and discuss. Thanks to David Duffy and Natalie Midgley for facilitating this, and to Euan and Tom at Brighouse for their co-operation during the following months; also to Sarah Rose in Halifax for her knowledge of where to look for information. Dave and Ian have also helped with the fascinating and diverting task of trawling through old copies of the *Brighouse Echo*, with occasional recourse to the *Halifax Courier*. Dave has been a constant source of encouragement, always willing to listen to me rambling on about the progress of the writing. He has also been first reader, scrutinising the manuscript at several stages of its evolution and making many important suggestions. Dave and I were brought up a few doors from each other next to the Stray, played on its acres as children, and have been friends for more than seventy years.

Chris Helme has been, as ever, a source of knowledge, resources, and support. Whenever I contact him with a question, he either knows the answer or has a document, stored in his loft, with the information. And he always knows exactly where to look. After a half-century of collecting I suspect Chris has extended his loft all the way around Holme Mews, above the bedrooms of his neighbours.

John Illingworth developed an interest in old postcards of Lightcliffe and district, visiting fairs when his son was searching for football cards in the final decade of the last century. He eventually had a collection of about 180 of these images. Many years ago he kindly donated this to the local history society. I have used several of these in the book, and speakers at our meetings have time and again showed slides taken from his images. They provide a fascinating portrait of our area in the first half of the twentieth century, especially its early years. I have used Malcolm Bull's *Calderdale Companion* many times when seeking biographical information on prominent characters of a century ago. It is an absorbing website and Malcolm has provided a valuable resource for local historians. John Millington's recollections of the Stray of his childhood, especially during the Second World War, have provided authentic first-hand accounts of the events of the time, and his meticulous local history notes are full of important detail. Others have helped with the loan of house deeds and photographs; they are acknowledged in the text. Where there is no acknowledgement, it is because the photographs have been in the local history society's gallery for a long time and I can't remember where they originated. Apologies to anyone not referenced.

Finally, thanks to The Amadeus Press, and in particular to Steve Waddington for his guidance and advice along the journey towards a final manuscript.

Notes on the Text

The following pages contain a variety of spellings of certain words. Firstly, with regard to place-names, these do evolve, although it is difficult to understand why this should happen in an age of mass literacy. For instance, the current spellings of Bailiff Bridge and Cliffe Hill are a reversal of those of a mere hundred years ago, when they were Bailiffe Bridge and Cliff Hill. We also have Lidgate and Lydgate. The earliest reference is 'Lydgate', in the 1529 'List of Gifts of Money towards Maintaining a Priest at Lightcliffe Chapel',[1] when Edmund Fairbank of 'Lydgate-in-Lightcliffe' donated 3s.4d. The spelling seems to have been 'Lidgate' in documents of the nineteenth century, reverting to 'Lydgate' by the time of *Illustrated Rambles* …[2] and the 1907 'Lydgate Estate' auction.[3] The house is now Lydgate House and the surrounding newer estate Lydgate Park. I have used the spellings appropriate to the period and the documents referred to. You will see the 'incorrect' versions of these and other nouns, proper and common, in direct quotes of council minutes or newspaper reports. My references throughout have been *New Hart's Rules* and the *Shorter Oxford Dictionary*.[4]

* * *

The book deals in old money: pounds, shillings and pence, or £.s.d. I originally included the decimal equivalents, for your guidance, in the text. However, there were so many they looked ungainly, so I deleted them. It's not difficult – a pound is a pound; there were twelve pennies to the shilling, twenty shillings to the pound. (On reflection, I think most potential readers will have a clear recollection of pre-decimal currency.)

* * *

In the Endnotes I have provided references to council meetings and newspapers only when they might otherwise have been unclear. Should anyone wish to follow up a reference, they have the month and year from the text.

* * *

You will notice that, although the predominant font is Adobe Garamond, the transcript of the Stray opening ceremony (Chapter 5) is in Times New Roman. This is because that was the font of the *Brighouse Echo* of 1923 from which the account is taken.

* * *

The William Faulkner epigraph is from his novel, *Requiem for a Nun*. The full quotation reads: 'The past is never dead. It's not even the past. All of us labor in webs spun long before we were born, webs of heredity and environment, of desire and consequence, of history and eternity.

---

[1] Parker, J., *Illustrated Rambles from Hipperholme to Tong* (Bradford, 1903), p.492.
[2] *Ibid, p.488.*
[3] See below, p.5.
[4] Waddingham, A. *New Hart's Rules: The Oxford Style Guide* (Oxford, 2014).

Contents

Illustrations

Chapter 4   Decision

Chapter 5   Opening Ceremony

Chapter 6   The Early Years – 1923-39

Chapter 7   World War Two

Chapter 8   Never Had It so Good

Chapter 9   Silver Jubilee Gala 1977

Epilogue

Endnotes

The past is never dead. It's not even the past.

William Faulkner

CHAPTER 1   SOME HISTORY

Samuel Washington Map 1820

SAMUEL WASHINGTON would be an almost anonymous figure in the story of Hipperholme and Lightcliffe were it not for the prominence his character received almost two centuries later in Sally Wainwright's television drama *Gentleman Jack*. In life, as in historical fiction, Washington was the land agent to Shibden Hall, having been appointed by Anne Lister in 1832 on the death of his predecessor, James Briggs. He already fulfilled that role for the Walkers of Crow Nest, subsequently combining the two.[1]

Washington was just twenty-three when, in 1820, he surveyed much of Hipperholme and part of Lightcliffe to produce the first large-scale map of our then sparsely populated villages. The field names were added in a survey book of 1837 and maps of 1840 and 1850, when Washington's plan was updated by George Hepworth.[2] The portion reproduced below (adapted by Peter Bottomley) shows that the area around Towngate was the centre of the community, other buildings few and isolated. There was no Leeds and Whitehall Road (A58) until 1833, and Sutherland Road was an even later creation. They have been added to show where the Stray would be situated. The horizontal road at the bottom is Wakefield Road, the one at the top Bramley Lane. These are linked by Denholmegate Road in the west and what is now Knowle Top Road in the east. (The latter was in fact a continuation of Bramley Lane at the time.) A portion of the fields to the north and west of Lidgate, shaded yellow, became the Memorial Stray a century later. The fields involved are Joan Ing, Back Laith Close, North Close, Lower Sour Ing, Upper Broad Close and Lower Broad Close, with a small portion of Knowl.

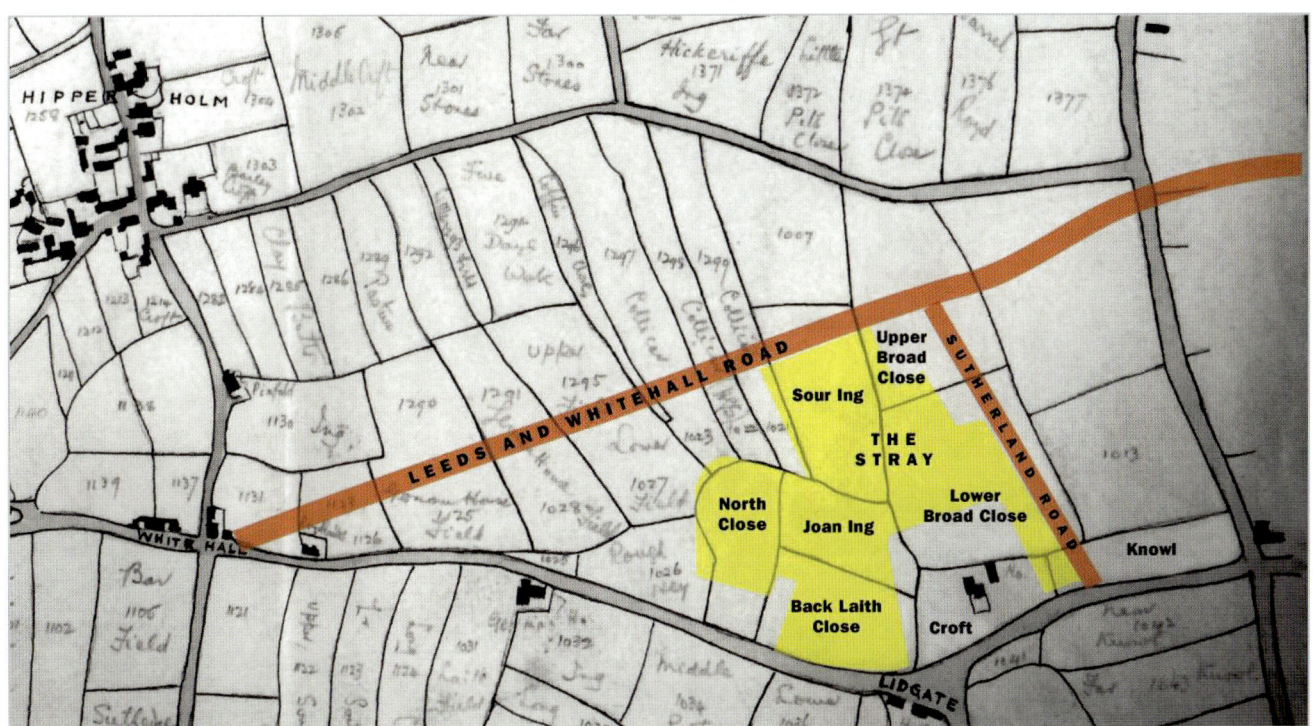

(Adapted by Peter Bottomley)

The owners of land, and we are speaking here of the appropriations and assumptions that began in Anglo-Saxon times but accelerated under Norman England, needed to identify their possessions, mainly for the purpose of charging and recording the payment of rents by their tenants. A distinct area of land acquired a name related to its dominant feature, such as agricultural use, size and location, the lie of the land, its soil, crops, livestock, wild animals and plants, buildings, land ownership. Pre-literate outdoor workers would be familiar with the variety of terms used to describe parcels of land in their locality.

'Close', meaning enclosure, is from a Middle English word, 'clos', derived from Old French. 'Croft', a familiar word, is a small close, or enclosure, usually next to a house. 'Ing', from an Old Norse word, is a meadow, especially one near water. The first word of a field-name almost always refers to an obvious characteristic. Thus, 'North' and 'Broad' are clear enough. A 'Laith' was a barn, so Back Laith Close presumably derives from the proximity of a farm building. 'Joan' would identify an owner, or former owner, or family member of an owner. The use of people's names is a common feature of English field-names.

'Sour' meant the state of being waterlogged, badly drained. Chris Helme brought to my attention the possibility that there was once a stream running through these fields.[3] The use of the word 'Ing' in two of the fields would support the assertion that it was at least marshy land, and to this day the area around the play equipment is boggy after heavy rain. Furthermore, the 1854 O.S. Map (*right*) identifies a 'Trough' at almost exactly the spot the Stray shelter later occupied, next to the current play area.

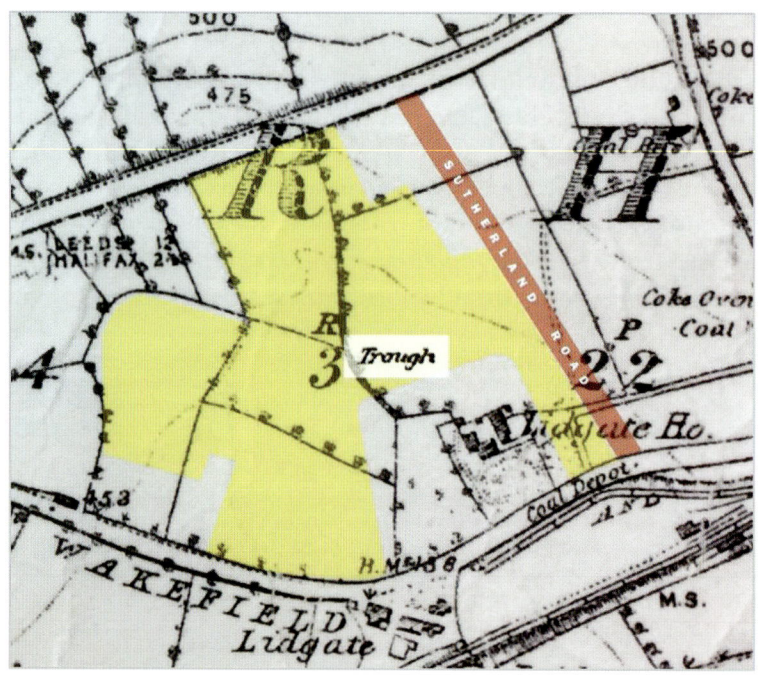

(Adapted by Peter Bottomley)

Crown Nest Sale 1867

The fields around Lidgate House (identified on the above map), and most of Lightcliffe and Bailiff Bridge, were part of the Crow Nest estate. On the death of her sister, Elizabeth Sutherland, in 1844, Ann Walker became sole owner of these lands and properties. She lived at Lidgate House for three or four years, and was visited there by Anne Lister, before, in 1834, Ann Walker joined her lover at Shibden Hall. Ann left the estate to her nephew, Evan Charles Sutherland, on condition that he added 'Walker' to his name. Ann died in 1854. Titus Salt was living at Crow Nest at the time, as a tenant. He remained there until 1858. Sutherland Walker moved to the mansion in the following year when he married Alice Sophia Tudor.

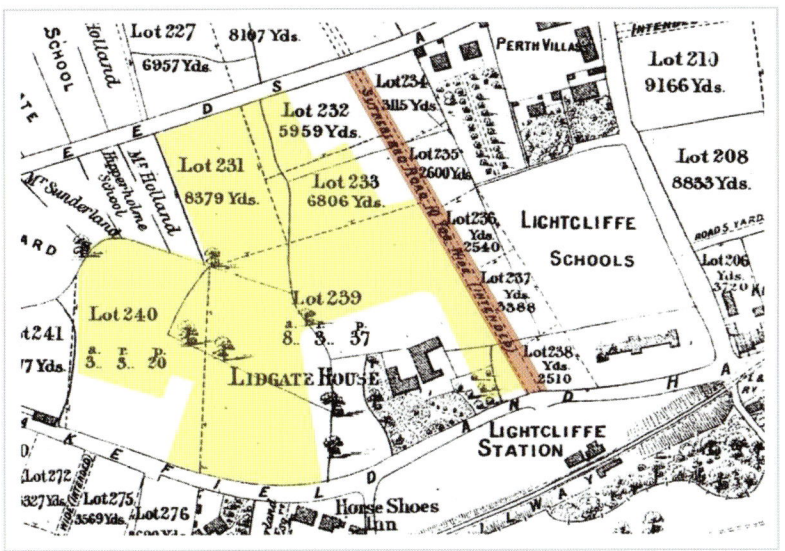

By the mid-1860s Sutherland Walker wanted to return to Scotland. He obtained an act of parliament, known as the 'Sutherland-Walker Estate Act', granting him permission to sell the estate.[4] To that end an auction was held in April 1867 at the New Assembly Rooms, Harrison Road, Halifax. The lots, including Lidgate House and what became the Stray, were tenanted by Joshua Smithson. The house was unsold after failing to meet the reserve price.

Extract from the map accompanying the 1867 auction schedule, land which would become the Stray again shaded yellow. *(Adapted by Peter Bottomley)*

The Smithson Family

In 1874 Joshua Smithson bought Lidgate House. He had already acquired some of the surrounding land, part of what became known as Smithson Park, according to the *Brighouse Echo* report of the auction proceedings.[5] However, another section of the park eventually came into the possession of his brother Joseph, fifteen years his junior.

Joshua Smithson *(right)* was born in 1817 in Port Patrick, Westmorland. He had four brothers, the youngest of which was Joseph, and two sisters. In 1841 Joshua was a tea dealer, living at Fountain Street, Halifax, with Thomas Collinson. (Remember Collinson's Tea Rooms?) In 1851 he lived at Gibbet Street with John, one of his younger brothers, also a tea dealer, and his sisters Elizabeth and Agnes. In 1855 Joshua married another Elizabeth. In the 1861 census he was still a tea dealer, but he and his wife were in Southport, possibly as visitors. It seems likely that the Smithsons moved into Lidgate House on the departure of Sutherland Walker, and they remained there in 1871 and 1881. From 1874 to 1881 he was the chairman of Hipperholme Local Board, the forerunner of the urban district council. Elizabeth died in 1888. Joshua continued to live at the house until his death in 1906. He had become a cotton manufacturer in the census returns for 1871, a bizarre change of occupation for a man in his fifties. This remained his line of business in the next three census returns.

(Chris Helme Collection)

Joseph Smithson, Joshua's brother *(left)*, lived with his family at Yew Trees, St. Giles Road. He was a stuff manufacturer (Joseph Smithson & Company) at Brunswick Mills, South Street, off West Parade, Halifax. Joseph moved into these premises in 1874, the year his brother bought the Lidgate estate. Were these purchases made possible through an acquisition of wealth by the Smithson family?[6]

(In the 1891 census Joseph is a widower. Living with him at 'Yew Cottage' are his four children, his 97-year-old mother, Agnes, his two sisters, Elizabeth and Agnes, a Housekeeper, Lady's Maid, Nurse, and Housemaid. On the day of the census they were also hosting a 'Visitor'.)

(Chris Helme Collection)

The plan to the right *(courtesy of Francis and Jo Stoker)* shows the joint ownership, in a deed of 1908, of the area which became the Stray, although individual plots alongside Sutherland Road and Wakefield Road were sold for building before the unveiling of the memorial in 1923. The two areas in different shades of blue had been in the possession of Joseph, and were inherited, on his death in March 1908, by his three sons: Joshua junior, Charles, and Joseph junior, and his son-in-law, James Arthur Jackson. A year earlier the three brothers had inherited from their Uncle Joshua the rest of the land (which included Lydgate House, not shown on the plan) bordered by Sutherland Road and Wakefield Road, marked 'Exors of Joshua Smithson decd.'. In a deed of 30 July 1908 ownership of the areas in blue was

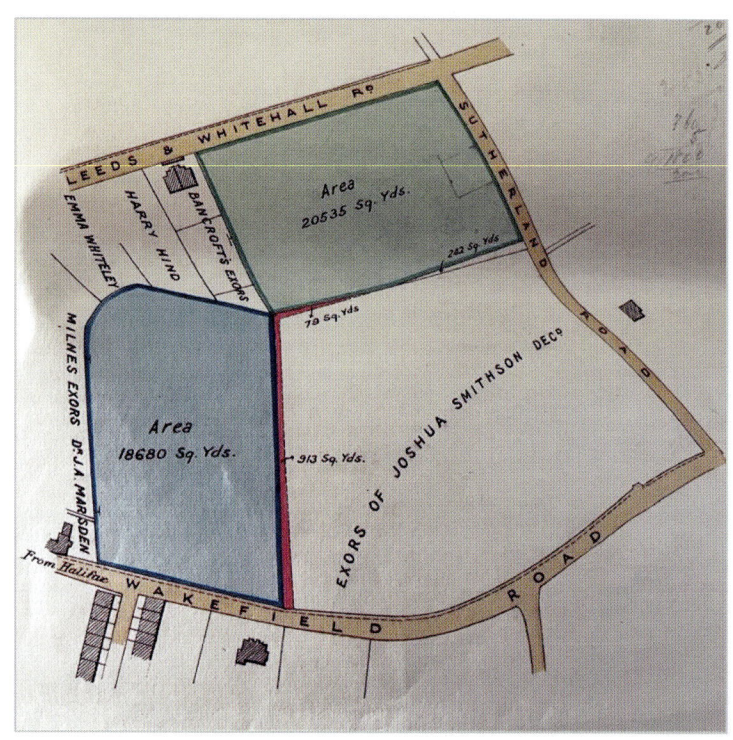

transferred from the three brothers and James Arthur Jackson to only two brothers, Charles Holmes Smithson and Joseph Smithson, thus excluding the oldest of the brothers, Joshua junior.[7] It was the brothers Charles and Joseph who eventually sold Smithson Park, which means that Joshua junior must also have transferred to his brothers his share in Lydgate House and the area marked 'Exors of Joshua Smithson decd.' in the above plan.[8]

(To allay any confusion: the older Joshua and Joseph Smithson were brothers. Joshua had no children, Joseph had three sons and a daughter. The three sons were Joshua, Charles and Joseph.)

Among the guests at the opening of the Stray in 1923 were 'Mr Joseph H. Smithson, J.P., and Mrs. Smithson, Mr. C. H. Smithson, J.P., and Mrs. Smithson'.[9] Joshua, the oldest of the brothers, lived until 1937 but he is not recorded as being present. In the 1911 census both Charles and Joseph are 'Directors' of 'Textile Manufacturers', while Joshua is a 'Dress Goods Manufacturer', but classed as 'Employed'. He is a 'Boarder' at 10, West Parade, Halifax, close to Brunswick Mills. He was thirty-nine. The owner of the house was a 43-year-old widow, Mary Duncan. Intriguingly, Joshua junior seems to have been written out of the family history.

Smithson Park Auction 1907

The Smithson brothers, as we have seen, had inherited on the death of their uncle. Joshua died on 14 December 1906. Probate was granted on 24 April 1907. Smithson Park was divided into lots and put up for auction at the Old Cock Hotel, Halifax, on Friday 10 May 1907 'at half-past seven o' clock in the evening', according to the *Brighouse Echo* of 3rd May. However, the brothers now owned only Lots 1 to 32 in the auction plan below. The remaining lots belonged to their father until the brothers inherited a year later. This means that father and sons together must have devised this housing scheme for the park.

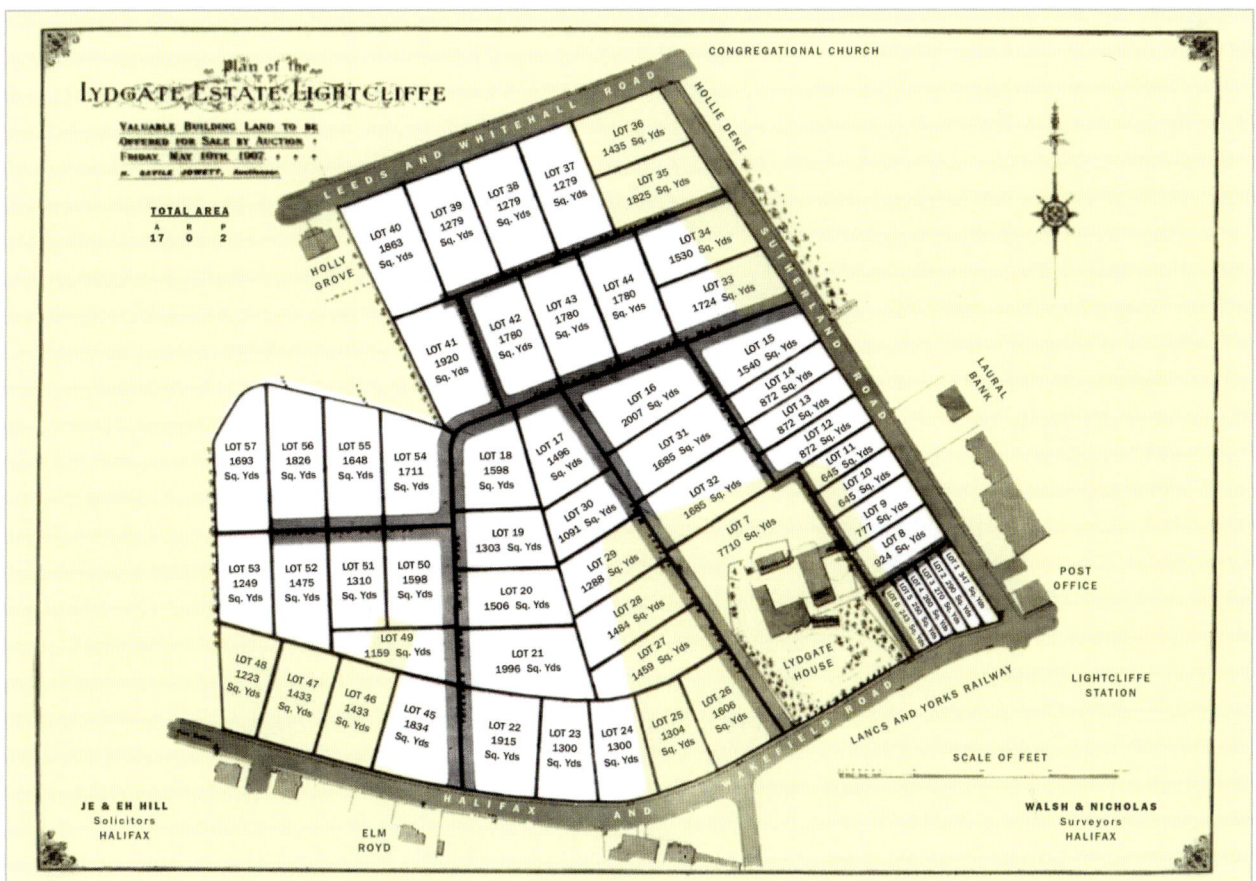

The unshaded (white) areas would become the Memorial Stray 16 years later.

(Auction plan adapted by Peter Bottomley)

There were fifty-eight lots, although number 58 does not appear on the plan. It was described in the notice as 'All those 3 FREEHOLD COTTAGES fronting to the Halifax and Wakefield Road, and situate near to the Liberal Club at Lightcliffe.' Hipperholme and Lightcliffe Liberal Club, at a cost of £1,000, was opened in 1881 by John Lister of Shibden Hall.[10] It was, for most of its post-political life, a school, best known as Lightcliffe High School before it became the junior section of Hipperholme Grammar School. It was also a British restaurant during the Second World War, serving inexpensive meals to families in difficulties. It has recently been demolished as part of the Watkins Close development. (Archibald Lionel Watkins was the founder and Head of Lightcliffe High School.)

Hipperholme and Lightcliffe Liberal Club   *(John Illingworth Collection)*

Lots 8 to 57 were building plots, described only by their acreage. Numbers 1 to 6 were advertised as 'Suitable sites for Shops and Dwellinghouses, with frontages of about 20 feet to the Halifax and Wakefield Road …' (They are the ones between Lydgate House and the post office.) Lot 7 was 'LYDGATE HOUSE and GROUNDS, comprising 3 kitchens, 4 reception rooms, 6 bedrooms and attics, 4-stall Stable, Carriage House, large Barn, Greenhouses and numerous Outhouses.'

The auction notice concluded with the information that 'The Estate is situated in a sheltered and favourite residential district, and all the surrounding property is a good class character. The Lightcliffe Parish Church, the Congregational Church, the Hipperholme Grammar School, the Halifax Tramways and the Lightcliffe and Hipperholme Railway Stations are all within a few minutes' walk of the centre of the property.'

There was a 'large attendance' at the Old Cock. It was suggested that interest had been aroused by two possibilities for use of the land: it could become a public park, or it might be 'suitable for development on "garden city" lines.' The reference to a park is intriguing: there is a world of financial difference between parkland and 58 housing lots. The auctioneer, H. Savile Jowett, referred to the low rates in this 'beautiful residential district'. At 6s.8d. in the pound, soon to be reduced to 6s.6d., they were half a crown (2s.6d. or 12½p) cheaper than Halifax, Bradford or Huddersfield.

Firstly, the whole estate was offered in one lot, but the highest bid, £1,700 from a Mr. C.T. Rhodes, was unacceptable. Lots 1 to 6 also received offers which were too low. Next came Lydgate House itself. There was no offer at all. After trying one or two building plots Mr. Jowett, frustration creeping in, exclaimed, "I'm tempting you. Is there no advance?" Buyers were invited to ask for special lots. There were no enquiries. Eventually, the only sale of the evening was made. Lot 58, the three cottages near to the Liberal club (they are now known as Green Mount), net rental £36 a year, were purchased for £500 by Hipperholme butcher Harold Sunderland. For many years he kept the shop at the corner of Leeds & Whitehall Road and Whitehall Street, now occupied by Anisa's Indian Takeaway.

There were no other bids. The auctioneer, either unrealistically optimistic or desperate to retain credibility, 'prophesied confidently that this bargain for builders would ultimately be sold.' He further suggested that the sale 'might not have been in vain; it was possible they would be inundated with buyers in the course of a few days.' He was wrong. The following year the three brothers inherited the remainder of Smithson Park on the death of their father, and lots 33-36 on Sutherland Road did sell, as did lots 46-48 (Netherfield and Rylstone) alongside Wakefield Road. However, there was to be no Smithson Garden City.

Smithson Park

(John Illingworth Collection)

7

The illustration on the previous page is entitled 'Smithson Park'. The original postcard is stamped 'Lightcliffe Post Office 30 April 1919', which might be a clue as to the date it was taken. It was sent to a Mr. & Mrs. Wolland of Newmarket, Cambridgeshire by one C. Byrne, who gave his/her address as c/o Mrs. Sellers. The Wollands were informed that, 'It's bitter cold here'. (In 1919 Charles and Alice Sellers lived at 45, Wakefield Road, one of the three cottages in Lot 58 of the 1907 auction.) The current names of the houses at the top of the park, on the west side of Sutherland Road (lots 33-36), are (from the right) Friars Crag, Meadow Crest (the bungalow demolished and replaced by a semi-detached two-storey dwelling), Lynton, Somerley and Field Head. All were built in the years following the 1907 auction. One of the Stray paths would follow the line of the fence in the photograph.

How long these fields had been known as Smithson Park is uncertain. When the possibility of purchasing them was first mentioned at a meeting of the of the Hipperholme Urban District Council on 9 September 1920, they were referred to as 'Lydgate Estate'. The chairman of the Council was authorised to interview Mr. Smithson (no indication as to which) and 'endeavour to obtain a firm offer with regard to the purchase of land at Lydgate Estate for War Memorial purposes.' However, the *Echo* report of a public meeting, held on 17 July 1919, to discuss memorial ideas (more of which later) referred to 'Smithson's Park'. As we shall see, it was two years before the suggestion was followed up, during which time other memorial options were considered. By the autumn of 1922 the land was referred to as 'Smithson's Estate' or 'Smithson's Park'.

(John Illingworth Collection)

I have mentioned the possibility that there was once a watercourse running across at least part of this pasture. The illustration opposite could support this contention. In the bottom left of the photograph there appears to be a depression, and perhaps a bridge, although this is not conclusive. Additionally, there is slight evidence of a path from the bridge heading beneath the trees.

The fence which continues from the potential bridge links with that in the Smithson Park photograph. One assumes that the building on the left behind the trees is a barn, although there is no building at this spot on any earlier or contemporary Ordnance Survey map. Finally, in the war memorial committee's closing accounts of June 1925 (see p. 57) there is an item £31.9s.5d. for the purchase of 'Earthenware Pipes'. These can only have been used for installing drainage, and there is surely nowhere else in the fields which were to become the Stray where drainage would be necessary.

Below is a view of an unmade Sutherland Road at about the time of the 1907 auction, taken earlier than the above illustration of the north-eastern corner of Smithson Park because there do not seem to be detached houses towards the top of the road on the left. What is evident from both photographs is the wall surrounding the park. Both these walls, alongside Leeds and Whitehall Road and Sutherland Road, were demolished as part of the creation of the Stray. Note also that Upper Sutherland Road is a narrow track rather than a thoroughfare.

SUTHERLAND ROAD LIGHTCLIFFE

The gas lamps would have been purchased from Halifax Corporation, which was possibly the only local authority to manufacture these pieces of industrial art.
(See 'Seating, Paths and Lighting' in Chapter 6, 'The Early Years – 1923-39'.)   *(John Illingworth Collection)*

THE JUNCTION
HIPPERHOLME

A contemporary view of Hipperholme crossroads. Note the recently laid tramlines in the foreground. On the left, adjoining the Whitehall Hotel, the sign reads 'Barker & Co. Auctioneers'. The sign at what is now Anisa's Takeaway is J. Sunderland & Sons. They were butchers. One of the sons, Harold, as we have seen (page 7), was the only person to make a successful bid at the 1907 Lydgate Estate auction. Between the Whitehall and the butcher, in the premises now occupied by Hipperholme News and Heavenly Harvests, was the village blacksmith.

(John Illingworth Collection)

CHAPTER 2   CELEBRATION AND COMMEMORATION

ON MONDAY 11 November 1918 the armistice was signed at Le Francport near Compiègne by the Allied Supreme Commander, Field Marshal Ferdinand Foch. Although it was signed at 5.45 a.m., it did not come in to force until 11 a.m. that morning.[11] The *Brighouse Echo* of four days later informs us that 'At Hipperholme the news was received with subdued exhilaration, because of the losses sustained in that district, but also with pride because it had contributed so much to the result. Bunting and flags were displayed in the streets, and at noon the church bells rang. The works in the district closed for the day.' St. Matthew's church was full on the Wednesday evening for a service of thanksgiving. The Rev. H. L. Taylor gave a short address, taking his text from Proverbs xxi, 31: 'The horse is prepared against the day of battle, but victory is of the Lord.' Which begs the question, to whom does defeat belong?[12] By the following summer 250 local men had been demobbed.

Priestley Green Hospital

The temporary military hospital at Holroyd House, Priestley Green, closed soon after the signing of the armistice. The house, owned by Sir Algernon and Lady Janet Firth, of the Bailiff Bridge carpet firm, had been opened as a convalescent home for injured servicemen in February 1917. During 1918, 445 patients had been admitted to its forty-eight beds. Lady Firth acted as commandant, with a matron, medical officer, sister, cook, three V.A.D. (Voluntary Aid Detachment) nurses, and from forty to fifty voluntary day helpers.

The road through Priestley Green would run behind the house, looking from this eastern perspective. The pond is still there.

(John Illingworth Collection)

Some of the 445 patients who were nursed at Priestley Green Hospital.   *(John Illingworth Collection)*

The income in 1918 had been £1,886.7s.5d. and expenditure £1,836. A meeting of subscribers decided that the Halifax Royal Infirmary and Lightcliffe District Nursing Association should receive gifts of 'linen etc.' Both organisations would benefit further after the sale of equipment. This took place in February 1919 at the offices of the auctioneer, Charles Wm. Laycock, at 11, George Street, Halifax. After the war Col. Robert H. Goldthorp lived at Holroyd House.[13]

Sir Algernon and Lady Janet Firth
(Chris Helme Collection)

Sir Algernon Firth (1856-1936) was the son of Thomas Freeman Firth, who started the carpet business, which became T. F. Firth and Sons Ltd., at Flush Mills in Heckmondwike in 1860. Seven years later he established the mill at Bailiff Bridge. Algernon became chairman of the company from 1909 until his retirement in 1921, when he was succeeded by his nephew, Sir William Aykroyd.

Algernon married Janet Gertrude Lindsay in 1881. They lived at Holme House, Lightcliffe, at the top of the hill out of Bailiff Bridge into Lightcliffe. He was High Sherriff of Yorkshire in 1922-23. Sir Algernon and Lady Janet were generous supporters of the community, donating George V Park and the drinking fountain at Bailiff Bridge in 1911. In 1917, as we have seen, they set up the military hospital at Holroyd House in Priestley Green, where Lady Janet was mentioned in despatches for her role as commandant of the military hospital. In retirement they moved to Knaresborough. It is said that when they left the area, people wept in the streets.

Sunny Vale Celebration

The armistice was extended three times during the continuing negotiations, before the Treaty of Versailles was eventually signed on 28 June 1919, exactly five years after the assassination of Archduke Franz Ferdinand, which led to the outbreak of war at the beginning of August 1914. There were more celebrations throughout the country. St. Matthew's church held a morning service and an evensong on Sunday 6th July. The earlier of these was a local civic thanksgiving and was preceded by a procession from the council offices, where the constables met. They marched along Leeds Road, to be joined at Knowle Top Road by the civic party, comprising many of the Hipperholme councillors. The following Friday the *Brighouse Echo* reported that 'The service was marked with a keen devotional spirit and the Vicar's sermon dealt with a peace on paper and an ideal peace founded on God's law.'

(John Illingworth Collection)

Hipperholme District Council organised festivities at Sunny Vale Pleasure Gardens, 'Sunny Bunces', for all the children in Hipperholme, Lightcliffe and Bailiff Bridge. The grounds were given up for the day, Saturday 19th July, by the Bunce brothers, James and George. Joseph, their father, the man who started the enterprise forty years earlier, had died the previous year. The Bunces' staff was augmented by volunteers: men on the gate, women in the tea room. It had been intended to include all local people in the festivities but it was decided to hold a separate event for the 'old folk'. It was felt that, as it was the holiday season, many would be away, and there was also concern that the lack of conveyances would mean the ancients faced a stiff uphill walk back to their homes at the end of the day.

The weather was 'glorious', according to the following Friday's *Echo*. More than 1,000 young people enjoyed the charity of the Council and the Bunces. All children under fourteen received a free tea and six penny tickets to be spent in the park. The Idle and Thackley Band played selections in the afternoon and accompanied the dancing in the evening. There was Professor Fay's Punch and Judy Show, 'the mysteries of Bert Turner, magician', the Helios Concert and Variety Company, but 'by far the most appreciated attraction was the Maypole dancing by the local children.' The dancers had been trained by George Hague, headmaster of Lightcliffe National Schools, and Ethel Womersley, a member of staff, along with other unnamed colleagues.[14] *The Echo* tells us that 'the day's celebrations were brought to a close by a wonderful and great display of fireworks, the like of which has scarcely been seen in the locality.'

The woman in white is Ethel Womersley, a legend at Lightcliffe Golf Club as well as in the classroom. I don't know the identity of her companions. They are in front of the first golf clubhouse. On the right, across Leeds and Whitehall Road, is the White Horse.
(Elizabeth Swallow Collection)

'Happy Day At Norwood Green'

The *Brighouse Echo* provides us with a headline for the Norwood Green event of three weeks later, Saturday 9th August, when 'the village … right royally celebrated the conclusion of the war and the signing of peace.' A procession gathered near the clock tower (then part of Norwood Green school, now housing) at the top of Village Street and marched to the cricket field.[15] It was headed by three of the village constables, followed by the Southowram Band; then came wounded and demobilised soldiers, and sailors and soldiers on leave, 'the village children attired in all sorts of fancy and comic costumes, and finally 'the elders … with two other special constables.'[16]

COPYRIGHT
NRD. G. 6

VILLAGE STREET, NORWOOD GREEN

LILYWHITE LTD.
BRIGHOUSE

(John Illingworth Collection)

The children, fifteen years and under, were given tea, coffee and buns and a quarter-pound packet of toffee. In addition, they received a gift to take home. The 'old folk over 60 years and widows' sat down to tea in the schoolroom. There was 'beef, ham, tongue … sweet loaves and cakes, buns of all descriptions … a spread rarely seen nowadays.' Those too unwell to attend had food taken to their homes. There were gifts for the elderly as well. 'The old ladies had half-a-pound of tea ... to take home, and each old gentleman two ounces of tobacco.' In all, more than 200 people, young and old, were catered for.

There was dancing and entertainment at the cricket field during the evening. The chairman of the parish council, E. W. Hanson, presented prizes and thanked the organisers, congratulating them on providing gifts for every child and old person in the village. 'The playing by the band of the National Anthem brought to a close one of the finest efforts made by the village.'

'Old Folk Entertained At Hipperholme'

The *Brighouse Echo* of 3 October 1919 reported an evening held at the Bramley Lane School on the previous Saturday, 29th September.

Bramley Lane School (*left, in 1973, from Leeds Road*) stood near the bottom of Bramley Lane on a site now occupied by a new bungalow, Bramley House. Built in 1823 as Bramley Lane Chapel (also known as Mount Zion) by the Primitive Methodists, it was sold three years later to the Independents or Congregationalists. It was used as a Sunday school until 1892, when a new school was built.[17] This is the Christ Church building, still in use, next to the former Congregational church, now occupied by private dentists. The old chapel / schoolroom was a military store during the Second World War, after which it was occupied by Vernon Moss Ltd., Electro Platers, until they moved to Churchfields Road, Brighouse, in the mid-1970s.

(Author's Collection.)

A group of councillors, joined by members of the long-established Old Folks' Treat Committee, organised the event, setting the age qualification at sixty years. They 'spared no effort to enable the aged guests to have a most enjoyable time.' Nearly 300 invitations were sent out and almost all were taken up. The committee was 'thoughtful in providing conveyances for the old folk who were not as nimble on their feet as in former years'. Newton Brooke, chairman of the Council until earlier in the year, 'very generously lent one of his motor cars for that purpose.'[18]

The tea was prepared and served by ladies whose surnames are recognisable as belonging also to members of the organising committee, all men. 'The repast won the hearts of the old folk at once; it was splendidly served, and was done full justice to by all.' At the conclusion of tea, the chairman of the Council, William C. Womersley, addressed the gathering.[19] This, he said, was the area's last celebration of peace. He drew a comparison with a year earlier when 'the armed strife touched almost every home', praising all for their self-sacrifice and for taking 'their share of the hardships with practically no grumbling or complaining'. He referred to the creation of 'a new walk from near the White Horse Inn to Bailiffe Bridge', which was the war memorial scheme being promoted by the Council. The announcement was greeted with applause.

The evening concluded with a concert, featuring a variety of singers, though it was Mr. H. McKenzie ('versatile entertainer') who 'captivated the hearts of the old folks with his witty songs.' The *Echo* concludes: 'During the concert light refreshments and tobacco were handed round amongst the old folk, and before leaving, each guest was presented with a quarter-pound of tea.'

Lightcliffe Congregational Church

The first memorial in our district was a commemorative tablet, unveiled at Lightcliffe Congregational church on Saturday, 3 September 1919. (Sir Titus Salt had been a substantial donor towards the cost of the building, which was opened in 1871.) On this occasion the church was 'almost full' for the thanksgiving service which followed the unveiling.[20]

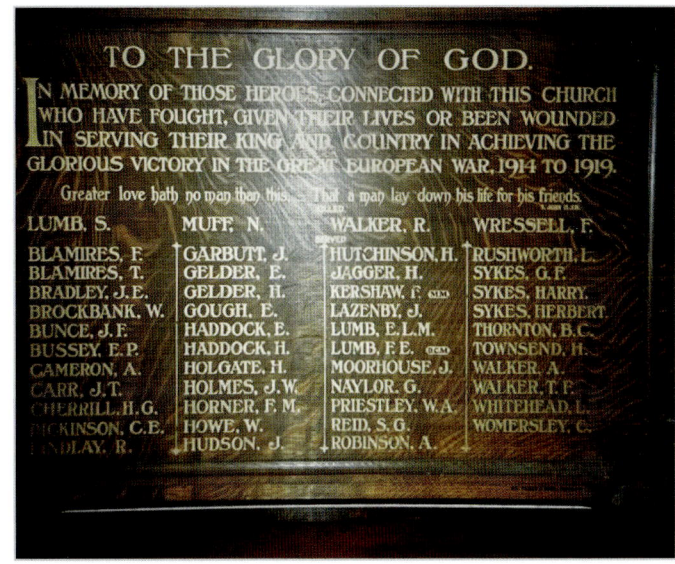

The ceremony was conducted by 'Brigadier-General E. N. Whitley, C.B., C.M.G., D.S.O., T.D., etc.'.[21] The minister, Rev. Frank Horrox,[22] introduced the 'distinguished officer' and thanked him for coming along at short notice. The minister explained that the tablet was intended to be part of a 'greater scheme'. They had hoped to have their bells re-hung 'so that they could ring forth in the peace celebrations' but the cost was beyond them for the time being. Rev. Horrox concluded by saying that they were 'met there to dedicate the memorial tablets to God to bear in memory those who laid down their lives for them, and also to accord a hearty welcome to the soldiers who had returned'.

Coley St John's

In the church of St. John the Baptist, Coley, there is a memorial tablet alongside the south aisle, containing the names of seventy-five parishioners who died in the First World War. It is a Hopton Wood white marble plaque within a black marble frame, and was the work of M. Noble of West Vale.[23] Mr. Noble also carved the memorials of Bailiff Bridge, Clifton, Norland, and Providence Congregational church, Stainland. The Coley memorial tablet was unveiled on 11 January 1920.

(Both illustrations Calderdale Libraries)

Norwood Green

At the 1919 annual Norwood Green Parish Council meeting a committee of councillors and local residents was set up to consider what form a commemoration should take. There was some delay before, at a June meeting, two suggestions were forthcoming. Firstly, 'the corner opposite Farrar's shop should be set out in gardens and a stone memorial suitably inscribed erected'.[24] Alternatively, 'part of the Common near the old pond be made into a park'.[25] The latter seemed to be the scheme preferred by the committee, although it was decided that estimates of the costs of each be obtained, after which 'the corner opposite Farrar's shop' was decided upon.

The Norwood Green war memorial was unveiled on Sunday, 11 November 1923, Armistice Day, by Col. R. E. Sugden, C.M.G., D.S.O., of Brighouse.[26] It was situated 'opposite Farrar's shop' at the junction of Rookes Lane and Village Street, on 'a small plot of ground presented by the firm of Messrs. John Walker, cloth manufacturers.' The names of the village's seventeen dead were inscribed. The service 'did not last long', we are told. There were two hymns, 'led by the combined choirs of Coley Church, Norwood Green Congregational Church and St. George's Church, Norwood Green'. Prayers were led by the vicar of Coley, Rev. G. T. Jowett, D.D., and a lesson read by Rev. A. W. Groom.

(John Illingworth Collection)

Col. Sugden was in command of a battalion on the front line when the armistice was announced five years earlier. His account of the soldiers' reaction is unsettling in its authenticity:

> 'Just before the Armistice [we] had been doing some hard fighting … and both sides had lost a large number of men … When the "cease fire" sounded, and the troops were told to stand fast, [we] did not start celebrations, but simply lay down and went to sleep. After that [we] proceeded to bury … about 75 of our comrades and 200 Germans.'

He echoed a frequent observation on relationships between soldiers during the war: 'Class distinctions did not exist, and there were no petty social problems.'[27] He continued, that they believed 'they were fighting a war to end war … so that the future generations might not know the horrors and trials of war.' He was not to know how ironic his words would prove to be. He concluded with his opinion that 'the value of a man's life was not to be reckoned by its length or by his social position, or by the amount of money he had been able to amass, but by the willingness with which he came forward to sacrifice all for his fellow men.'

The memorial was dedicated by Dr. Jowett. Sergeant Thomas Wardingley 'sounded the mournful notes of the "Last Post" and, after one minute's silence, the ringing challenge of the "Reveille" was heard.'[28] The deeds were handed over by Councillor J. B. Carter, secretary of the war memorial committee, to the chairman of the Council, Councillor A. E. Wood. Proceedings were closed with the singing of the national anthem. Several wreaths were laid. I include only one dedication: 'In loving memory of Pte. Frank Holmes, from Miss Dalby.' So much unsaid.

Bugler Wardingley   (Author's Collection)

Bailiff Bridge

In June 1919 Mr. and Mrs. William Henry Aykroyd presented to the Hipperholme District Council a scheme to develop a plot of land they had recently purchased, adjoining Bailiff Bridge School.[29] They proposed to create an 'attractive garden' and erect an 'artistic memorial' to the sixty-one villagers, and employees of T. F. Firth & Sons, who had lost their lives. These included those who worked at Flush Mills, Heckmondwike, where the Firth carpet business started in 1860. The Aykroyds' two sons had joined up in August 1914, Major Alfred in the Royal Fleet Auxiliary and Captain Harold in the First-4th Duke of Wellington's. Both had served in France, and returned safely home.

The crowd at Bailiff Bridge. The hill in the left background, 'Jasper' to later generations, is marked 'Light Cliff' on early O.S. maps.   (Chris Helme Collection)

Less than two years later, on Saturday 2 April 1921, the Aykroyds' scheme came to fruition. William had now become Sir William, having received his baronetcy in the King's birthday honours in June 1920.[30] He had also become chairman of the directors of T. F. Firth & Sons in succession to his uncle, Sir Algernon Firth, and Alfred and Harold were now directors of the company. Both would become chairmen in future years. They had also resumed playing cricket for Lightcliffe in the Yorkshire Council.

The spring day was cloudless. The *Echo* records that 'the sun shone in benediction over the whole proceedings'. A large crowd was delighted at the sight of 'a most beautiful pleasure garden, in the centre of which stands … a magnificently proportioned cenotaph'. This had been designed by the architects Walsh and Maddock and sculpted by Caldwell Spruce of Leeds.[31] The lettering was, as we have seen, carved by M. Noble of West Vale, a busy man during these years. Amongst the dignitaries were Brigadier-General E. N. Whitley (see 'Lightcliffe Congregational Church', p.17), Sir G. A. Armytage,[32], Colonel R. H. Goldthorp, , and council chairman William Womersley. The chief guest, who performed the unveiling, was Field Marshall Sir William Robertson, described by the *Echo* as 'a war-worn veteran'.[33] Robertson is the only soldier in the history of the British Army to have risen from an enlisted rank to its highest rank of field marshal. There was the Bishop of Wakefield, The Right Rev. George Rodney Eden, a descendant of the eighteenth-century naval hero Admiral Rodney, after whom he was named. All local churches were represented. A guard of honour was provided by the 4th West Riding Regiment, under the command, for this occasion, of Captain Harold Aykroyd.[34]

There are two citations on the cenotaph, in addition to three panels containing the names of those who died. The citations read as follows:

In thankfulness for Victory, for Peace Restored, and for the lives of those returned from the War in safety, this Garden was presented to the people of Bailiffe Bridge by Sir William and Lady Aykroyd of Cliffe Hill —A.D.1921

1914   *1919*
To the Glorious Memory of the Men from Bailiffe Bridge and those who worked at Clifton and Victoria Mills, also Flush Mills, Heckmondwike, who, in the Great War, fought, fell and conquered, this monument was erected by Sir Willam and Lady Aykroyd, of Cliffe Hill, Lightcliffe – A.D. 1921

Buglers sounded a general salute as Field Marshall Robertson entered the park for the service, which was led by the bishop. Clifton Brass Band played Chopin's *Marche Funebre*. There were hymns, the singing led by the combined choirs of St Matthew's, Lightcliffe, St Aidan's Mission, Bailiff Bridge, and Ebenezer United Methodists, Bailiff Bridge.

The assembled chanted together the 23rd Psalm, which was followed by the bishop reading from the Book of Wisdom, chapter 3, verses 1-9. Verse 8 reads: 'They all hold swords, being expert in war: every man hath his sword upon his thigh because of fear in the night.'

The first address was given by Sir William himself. He began by reading a letter from Sir Algernon and Lady Firth regretting that they could not be present as they were in the south of France. They expressed their 'admiration and gratitude for the devotion to their country … of those who have fallen, and our deep sympathy with those who mourn their loss.' Sir William continued: 'They were men like ourselves, very human it may be, with many faults and failings, but men who, despite everything, accomplished great things because they saw clearly that to accomplish anything great a man must forget himself, face the worst that can come without flinching, and fight it to the end, though in the fight he himself goes down.' Sir William concluded by reading out the sixty-one names on the memorial. It is difficult to imagine the emotions of family and friends as an all too familiar name was sounded.

Sir William speaks to the gathering. On the left are the Bishop of Wakefield and Lady Aykroyd. Behind Sir William is Field Marshall Sir William Robertson. (Chris Helme Collection)

Field Marshall Sir William Robertson then spoke. He said that 'the war was won in the only way it could be won, by all classes of the nation holding together.' He gave a detailed history of the fluctuations of the campaigns, praising the resilience of British soldiers, which had taught him a lesson he would never forget: 'I was convinced there is good in every man – even in the most unpromising quarter.' But he asked if they were better for the terrible loss of life and the suffering. 'There is industrial unrest, discontent and unemployment. People are desirous of doing as little as possible, and getting as much as possible.' He called on those present to live up to 'the lofty spirit of selflessness' exemplified by the men whose names were on the memorial, which he hoped would serve as a continuing inspiration for the future. The field marshal then unveiled the monument, the union flag was raised, and the flags at Clifton and Victoria Mills, which had been at half-mast during the ceremony, were hoisted to full mast. 'Then came the clear, solemn notes of the "Last Post" and, after a moment's silence, the cheery notes of the "Reveille" were heard, these being sounded by Bugler Wardingley.' The bishop then dedicated the memorial, following which the band played the national anthem. The final act in proceedings provided 'one of the most moving incidents of the day' when relatives of the deceased laid wreaths at the cenotaph.

The Bishop of Wakefield and Field Marshal Robertson leave the ceremony. (Chris Helme Collection)

Joseph Wood & Sons Ltd.

Woods Mill, at the bottom of Badger Lane, Hipperholme (alongside the ancient highway known as Wakefield Gate) was built in the late 1840s as a steam-powered mill, spinning worsted yarn. By the end of the First World War the premises had been expanded and they had started producing specialist yarns. Regarding their memorial, I can do no better than quote in full the *Brighouse Echo* of Friday, 12 December 1919.

'An interesting ceremony, which greatly manifested the spirit and feeling of old friends, took place at the works of Messrs. Joseph Wood and Sons, Ltd., at Hipperholme Mills, on Saturday morning last. During the war many of the firm's employees joined up, five of them making the great sacrifice, and in appreciation of their services the employees have subscribed for and erected a clock and tablet over the office door. The unveiling ceremony was performed by Mr. Joseph Wood, a director of the firm, who gave a short address, and the clock was set in motion by Miss Susan Mallinson, who has been with the firm for 49 years. A few appropriate words were also spoken by Mr. E. H. Knowles, the manager of the works.'

Joseph Wood was a son of the founder of the company. The mill was demolished in 1969. All efforts to locate the clock and tablet have come to nought.

Hipperholme Grammar School

Generations of H.G.S. pupils, all boys until 1985, have stood every morning in school assembly and looked towards the memorial at the back of the stage. The names of former pupils who lost their lives in both wars are recorded, with prominence given to Maynard Percy Andrews, headmaster from 1911.[35] On 20 June 1919 the school's memorial committee met, under the chairmanship of John Lister of Shibden Hall, who was also chairman of the school governors.[36] The memorial tablet was already in place but the committee was anxious that it should contain a complete list. Through the newspaper columns they appealed for assistance from anyone who might have information.[37]

On 11 November 1920 the memorial (*right, courtesy of Calderdale Libraries*) was unveiled, containing the names in the top half, those lost in the First World War. The citation and carved image commemorate Maynard Andrews.

John Lister chaired the proceedings, accompanied on the stage by Dr. G. T. Jowett, the vicar of Coley, headmaster J. Kemp, and Major E. P. Chambers, clerk to the governors. Mr. Lister reminded the schoolboys of the sacrifices made by the master, assistant masters and old boys who 'gave their lives for the country.' He was followed by Major Chambers, who spoke of Captain Andrews, with whom he was serving at the time of his death, quoting their colonel, who said they had lost one of the best officers of the regiment. Chambers also quoted the inscription on another monument, for those who had died during the Boer War at the Battle of Wagon Hill in 1900: 'Tell England, ye who pass this monument, we who died serving her rest here content.' I don't wish to be disrespectful to one who knew at first hand the horrors of the First World War, but this seems to me an absurd euphemism. Perhaps such sentiments brought consolation to the surviving families. I hope so.

There is also a memorial on the front gate, leading from Bramley Lane into the oldest part of the school. The clock tower is actually on the building at the far side of the yard, which houses the room in which the novelist Laurence Sterne, prime minister Sir Robert Peel, and others, received part of their education.

(Author's Collection)

St Matthew's Church

'Unveiling Ceremony At Lightcliffe' was the *Brighouse Echo* headline as it reported the dedication festival of a church memorial to the men of the parish who lost their lives in the war.[38] The 'crowded congregation' included members of the Hipperholme District Council, and the boy scout troops of Brighouse, Bailiff Bridge and Rastrick. The Rev. H. L. Taylor conducted the service, which took place after evensong. It was preceded by the choir and clergy (the vicars of Halifax, Coley and Lightcliffe Congregational Church, and the Brighouse curate were also present) marching to the memorial at the west end of the church during the singing of the hymn 'Soldiers who are Christ's below.'

The memorial was designed by Harry Percy Jackson, the renowned Coley woodcarver.[39] The work was probably done by Jackson senior, although his son, also Harry Percy, born in 1896, had by this time followed his father into the business. Joinery work was carried out by Harry Gough.

The newspaper has the following detailed description, clearly taken from a programme of the event:

The memorial consists of church wardens' and sidesmen's seats, which flank the tablet of names of the fallen. The screen extends over the whole west wall of the church, and is in Gothic style, in keeping with the C15th. century style of the church. The tablet itself is crowned with a beautiful canopy, and the panel at the back is enriched with carved traceries. A cove and overhanging cornice is one of fine dignified design, with hanging traceries and double-membered carved moles, and finishing with beautiful pierced cresting. A handsome feature of the cornice is a cross reaching high in front of the west window, carrying a wreath of laurel and a terminal pendant, poised over the tablet, of carved cherubs, with crossed wings.

Knowle Top Road in 1914 or 1916. (It's difficult to read the date on the postcard.) Harry Gough's workshop is on the right behind the first telegraph pole, where Knowle Top Drive would be built in the 1930s. The car outside Knowl House probably belonged to Dr. John Gatherer Brown. (John Illingworth Collection)

Harry Percy Jackson (left) at the gate of his Morriscot home.

When the party was assembled, Major Goldthorp addressed Sir George Armytage: "Sir, in the name of the congregation, parishioners and friends of St. Matthew's, Lightcliffe, I ask you to unveil this memorial in grateful memory of those from this parish who lost their lives in the great war." Sir George drew back the union flag covering the memorial, after which he addressed the gathering. He asked them to cast their minds back seven years, when the largest army ever formed in this country was put together 'from all classes, all professions, all trades', augmented by 'men … from overseas little knowing what they would have to do.' Men from the parish were in twenty-eight different regiments and the 'gave their all for the country they loved.' He talked about the 'comradeship and loyalty' of those times and continued, "I want you to think what these men whose names we are commemorating would have thought had they come home … Are you all doing what they did and what they would have expected you to do? Are you being unselfish and working all you can to keep the peace … They wanted England to be a free country and a better country than when they left. I leave this thought with you."

The carving by Harry Jackson in St. Matthew's Church. A full list of names is contained in Appendix 1.

(Author's Collection)

The fine rhetoric of these occasions makes no reference to the view that, firstly, the war was only inevitable because of the imperialism of Great Britain, Germany and France, and, secondly, from the British point of view, there have always been accusations that the campaign was badly managed, that the British infantry were 'lions led by donkeys'.[40] To be fair, this opinion is not shared by all historians. However, nine million soldiers and five million civilians died, and twenty-three million were wounded. Middle-aged men missing an arm or a leg were not an uncommon sight in my childhood. Too young to understand, I assumed this was the natural order if things.

CHAPTER 3

DELIBERATION

HIPPERHOLME URBAN DISTRICT PEACE CELEBRATION.

A PUBLIC MEETING

Will be held

In the NATIONAL SCHOOL, KNOWL TOP,

On THURSDAY, JULY 17th, at 7-30,

to decide the form of Memorial to the Men who have fallen in the Country's cause and to those who have served.

For JULY 19th, the Council have already secured SUNNY VALE GARDENS, and through the kindness of Messrs. Bunce arranged for ENTERTAINING THE CHILDREN AND OLD FOLK of the District. Full particulars will be issued later.

A MEETING for the ENROLMENT of VOLUNTARY WORKERS will be held on MONDAY, JULY 14th, at the COUNCIL OFFICES.

Signed on behalf of the Council,

W. C. WOMERSLEY, Chairman.

ON 16 MAY 1919 the notice on the left appeared in the *Brighouse Echo*.

We have dealt with the successful Sunny Vale Gardens celebration, but what of the creation of a permanent memorial? The morning after this national school gathering (such was once the quality of local journalism) the *Echo* ran a headline, 'A War Memorial: Little Interest at Hipperholme', followed by a full account of the progress of the meeting. There was 'a very poor attendance'. William Womersley, chairman of the Council, outlined a twofold proposal. Firstly, there should be 'a new walk from Leeds and Whitehall Road down to Dog Bridge [see map on p.30] at the entrance of which ... there should be a monument ... bearing the names of all the men of the district who had fallen.' Secondly, he suggested a new recreation ground 'at the top end of Hipperholme'. The cost had been estimated at 'about £1,200 to £1,500'.

Further, he was pleased to say that 'the scheme met the approval of Sir Algernon Firth, Mr. W. H. Aykroyd, Mr. Newton Brooke and other influential residents.' One of the social effects of the war was supposed to have been a breaking down of class barriers: rich and poor had fought side by side; now they should live side by side. However, inherited wealth and status apparently still conferred the mark of plausibility.

There were other suggestions put forward at the meeting. The idea that Smithson Park would be a more central memorial came from an unidentified and prescient source. The erection of swimming baths or a library were also considered. Two members recommended that the most important concern should be 'the financial assistance of those widows and maimed soldiers who were receiving altogether inadequate maintenance from the State.' The outcome was that 'after much discussion it was decided to appoint a committee ... to go into the various schemes ... and report to a further meeting.' This was the Hipperholme War Memorial Committee. Four members of the community, presumably present at the meeting, were to be joined by four councillors. The local residents were Frances Wakefield, W. Brown, A. Bailey and Joseph Walsh. At a meeting of the General Purposes Committee later in the month, it was decided that the four councillors would be Algernon Denham, Lumb, Mallinson and Herbert Womersley, with chairman William Womersley as convenor.[41] Thus, the Council, which had proposed the walk and recreation ground scheme, had a majority.

The committee met on 2nd September.[42] 'Things are moving', reported our local newspaper, then sought to justify the apparent dilatoriness. Hipperholme people 'are quite as patriotic as people in other districts, and there is no doubt that they will loyally respond to the memorial once a scheme is definitely fixed.' The Council's twofold idea is again described in full, and the report concludes that this 'would make a most suitable memorial, and would not be so costly as some of the memorials suggested by individuals at the public meeting. Further developments are awaited.' The following week's *Echo* confirmed that the committee, with one dissenter, proposed the 'walk from White Horse Hill to Bailiffe Bridge' and the 'provision of a recreation ground' should be recommended to the Council, in the hope of 'their wholehearted co-operation so that the memorial scheme might be brought to a successful issue.' As the idea had originally been put forward by the Council at the July public meeting, there was little doubt the decision would be ratified.

Land at Hipperholme

Nothing further was mentioned about the Council's and war memorial committee's proposal in either Hipperholme council minutes or the local press. However, Chris Helme has a sequence of correspondence on the matter which took place in early 1920 between Newton Brooke, landowner and recent chairman of the Council, and Joseph Frederick Walsh, civilian member of the war memorial committee. It is unclear whether Brooke is acting privately or on behalf of Brookes Ltd.

The correspondence begins with what is apparently an internal memo (unsigned), dated 26 January 1920, summarising a meeting that day between Walsh and Brooke concerning 'negotiations for the purchase of land for recreation ground at Hipperholme (near tunnel).' There has only been one railway tunnel at Hipperholme, from east of Brighouse Road to the old Hipperholme station, near the Travellers Inn. Brookes Ltd.'s land came up to the railway line on the south side, between St. Giles Road and Brighouse Road, so this could have been the area the Council had in mind for a recreation ground. Walsh and Brooke had evidently agreed a value of £419 for the land. Walsh asked if Brooke would accept £300. Brooke said he would sell for £400 but would donate £100 'to the project'. Walsh agreed to put this to his chairman, presumably William Womersley. However, the memo also points out that Walsh has miscalculated the value of the 4795 square yards at two shillings per yard. It should have been £479. On the same day Brooke writes to Walsh informing him of this discrepancy. He says that he allowed £19 to bring the value down to £400; he will now allow £29 to bring it down to £450. He asks Walsh to ring him about the matter.

This promissory note, also dated the 26th, was obviously written by Brooke during the meeting as it values the land at £419, for which he will accept £400. (The scrawls at the top and bottom are shorthand. If anyone can decipher them, please let me know.)

HUDC top left. 'Mr J F Walsh' written beneath 'Brookes'   (Chris Helme Collection)

On 3rd February Walsh replied to Brooke's home address, asking if there could be a reduction as he fears 'the matter will fall through at the price you ask.' The following day Brooke responds that 'the price quoted is a reasonable one', but, anxious to reach agreement with the committee, he will reduce it by £50. He repeats his offer of £100 to what he now refers to as the 'Memorial Fund'. It would seem, therefore, that public subscriptions to the memorial walk / recreation ground scheme were already being sought.

Memorial Footpath

In a letter of 28 January 1920 Walsh acknowledges Brooke's offer to donate £100 to the Memorial Fund, but also introduces a further issue relating to the 'proposed Memorial Footpath at Lightcliffe'. He encloses a 'rough plan' and mentions that the route 'crosses the rough land at the bottom of one of your fields near the viaduct', continuing 'Sir Algernon Firth has given his consent as far as his property is concerned and I shall be greatly obliged if you can see your way to do the same.' How could mere Mr. Brooke refuse when a knight of the realm had agreed that the footpath could cross his land? In an undated and unaddressed letter, which seems to form part of this correspondence, Walsh gives a detailed description, transcribed below, of the proposed course of the footpath.

'Suggested War Memorial for Hipperholme'

'To acquire the rights to construct and maintain a public Footpath from the Leeds and Whitehall Road at Helliwell Syke, through the wood and fields under the viaducts to Dog Bridge as shown upon the Map.

To erect a Memorial Cross at the entrance from the Leeds and Whitehall Road. This would stand in a recess and have inscribed upon it the names of the Fallen.

The footpath from the road to the stream to be formed 8 feet wide with steps at intervals, in an avenue of Trees.

The wood to be entered on the North side of the stream, by easy steps and inclined path.

The Waterfall at the head of the stream to be restored so that the water runs evenly over the top, and the mound of the right hand side cleared in order to give a full view of the fall, at the foot of which a pool would be made.

The Footpath to continue on the North side of the stream, and continuing its irregular line, being formed of digging and filling with boulders on the lower side to retain same.

The Path would continue across the Field No. 42. on the Ordnance Map, past the Spa Well, which might be made a feature of by the erection of a drinking well, and continuing through the field belonging to the Exors. of the late Mr. John Pickles, crossing the Coley Beck by a Bridge, near its junction with Helliwell Syke, and under the Railway viaduct, past the Golf Green through the land coloured yellow on plan, and belonging to the Halifax Commercial Banking Company, and following Bottom Hall Beck across Till Carr Lane by the Ford, after which it would enter the land belonging to

Tolson's Exors. & coloured green, and again crossing the stream by a stone bridge into the field coloured purple and belonging to the Exors. of the late Sir Henry Ripley, terminating at Dog Bridge, a total length of ¾ of a mile.'

Walsh's 'rough plan' has not survived, but we have Peter Bottomley's polished reconstruction, based on the 1922 O.S. Map.

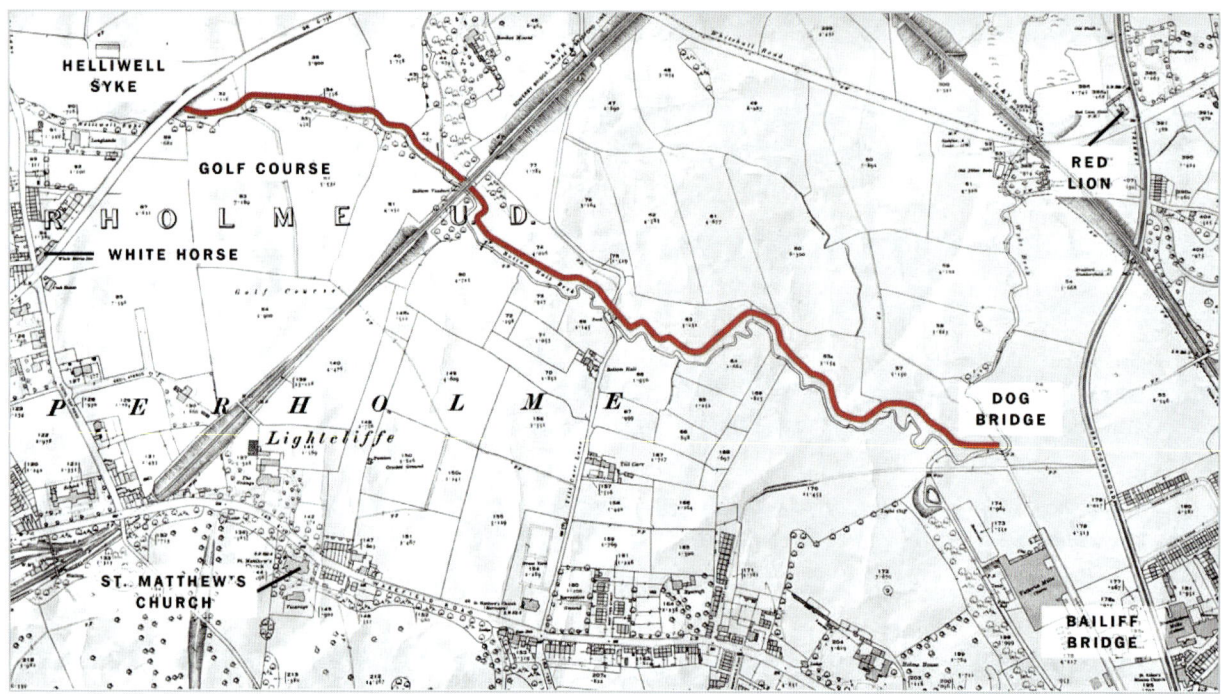

Walsh, presumably acting on behalf of the war memorial committee, had thoroughly surveyed the proposed route, evidence of the seriousness of the twofold proposal. It would seem that there was no obstacle to the purchase of land for a recreation ground at Hipperholme 'near tunnel', and that the viability of the footpath route depended only on Newton Brooke's permission for the route to cross 'rough land' near the viaduct. There is no record of a response from Brooke. Walsh, in a brief letter of 12th February, thanks Brooke for the reduction of £50 in the price asked for the Hipperholme land, adding that he would 'be pleased to hear from you respecting the Footpath below the Viaducts.'[43]

Why is there no further reference to this memorial scheme in Hipperholme District Council minutes, the *Brighouse Echo*, or extant correspondence? At a full council meeting on 9 March 1920, only a month later, the following decision was taken:

> **490. Land at Lydgate Estate.**
> Moved by Councillor DENHAM,
> Seconded by Councillor H. WOMERSLEY,
> That the Chairman of the Council interview Mr. Smithson re above and endeavour to obtain a firm offer with regard to the purchase of land at Lydgate Estate for War Memorial purposes. Carried.

What had happened in the few weeks since Walsh asked Brooke for permission to route the proposed footpath across his land? Councillors Denham and H. Womersley were both members of the war memorial committee so would presumably have been aware of the negotiations between the two, yet here they are promoting an entirely different scheme. (You will recall that the purchase of 'Smithson's Park' had been suggested at the public meeting the previous July. Is it reasonable to infer that the Smithson option had been discussed in the meantime, and favoured, by local people?) Equally strange is the fact that there is to be no further reference to the Smithson Park negotiations until October 1922, two-and-a-half years later, although, as will become clear, that might be partly due to the time it took to reach agreement with the Smithson brothers.

The offices of Hipperholme Urban District Council in the early years of the twentieth century.

Hipperholme U.D.C. replaced the Hipperholme Local Board in 1894 as manager of the affairs of Hipperholme, Lightcliffe and Bailiff Bridge. Initially it met at the Congregational church schoolroom until, in 1899, it was able to move into its own premises at the end of the row of shops in the centre of the village. The building was designed by Joseph Walsh, an influential and seemingly ubiquitous figure in local life. It was opened on 3rd August and included a council chamber, committee room, and a surveyor's house. Newton Brooke, later to be a councillor, and chairman of the Council, assisted in the acquisition of the land. It is not clear whether the land was actually in his ownership.

For forty-two years many aspects of local life were controlled by a succession of local men (there were just two co-opted women councillors during this time) who knew each other well and were familiar to all in the community. In 1937 its powers were taken over by Brighouse Council. The council chamber, on the first floor of the offices, became a public library, while a variety of businesses occupied the ground floor rooms. Principal amongst these was Martins Bank, which was eventually taken over by Barclays. In 2023 the library has closed, the businesses have gone, and, at the time of writing, it is the subject of a planning application to change the use to nine apartments.

The opening of the council offices on 3rd August 1899.

(John Illingworth Collection)

CHAPTER 4

DECISION

Negotiations

ON 20 OCTOBER 1922 Francis Marriner Horner, clerk to Hipperholme U.D.C., wrote to Newton Brooke, on behalf of the chairman of the Council, inviting him to meet members 'to discuss a matter of considerable importance'.[44] He added that the Council 'would be glad of your counsel and advice as the matter is one affecting the future welfare of the District.' It was further cryptically requested that 'this letter shall be regarded as private and confidential for the time being.' Three days later Brooke replied that another urgent engagement would keep him away from the meeting, but he would be happy to speak by phone if the clerk cared to ring him. He added that his number was 'Hipperholme 1'. Further, in a postscript, he almost implored the clerk to contact him by telephone. A record of the contact between Brooke and the Council ends there. He didn't own any of the land the Council hoped to acquire, nor had he been a member of the Council since he relinquished the chairmanship in 1919, which makes it difficult to understand why his involvement was evidently so important.

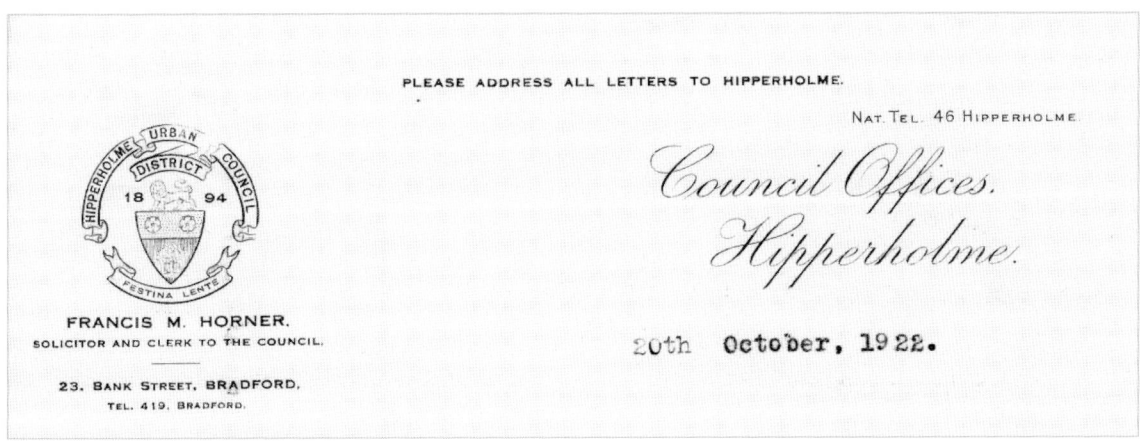

The Hipperholme District Council's letterhead. Note the telephone number, top right, and the council logo, with its maxim 'Festina Lente' – 'Make Haste Slowly'. The logo was taken up by Lightcliffe Cricket Club on the dissolution of the Council. Both logo and maxim have now been appropriated by Lightcliffe & District Local History Society.
(Chris Helme Collection)

The *Brighouse Echo* of 25 November 1921 contained an update on local war memorials. Bailiff Bridge, Brighouse and Elland were covered but there was no mention of progress in the Hipperholme project. It was almost twelve months later that copies of the notice overleaf were distributed around neighbourhood shops and other premises.

This notice was supported in the *Echo* of the 27th of October, under the heading 'A Hipperholme Park'. The article begins with a reference to the long delay but suggests that the Hipperholme district is likely to benefit from this as the 'prospect of purchasing Smithson's Estate of 11½ acres and adapting and using it as a public park' has arisen. We are told that 'a number of gentlemen who are prominently concerned with the welfare of the district have moved quickly in the interests of the community.' Two-

and-a-half years? Quickly? Why has it taken so long for prominent local gentlemen and the Smithson brothers to reach agreement?

The park, we are told, is to be 'a memorial in connection with the war', with open access at all times, similar to the Harrogate Stray. It will contain a monument, 'a big piece of Aberdeen granite, on which the names of the fallen soldiers could be inscribed'. The scheme has evidently been publicised locally and 'is likely to commend itself to the residents of the Hipperholme district', especially as the land is available at 'such an exceedingly reasonable figure.' It is intended that the purchase price be raised by public subscription, 'towards which generous support is already promised'. (It will be recalled that, in January 1920, Newton Brooke had offered £100 to the 'Memorial Fund'.) The Council undertakes to maintain the park. Finally, there is the assurance that 'Residents in the Hipperholme district will owe a debt of gratitude to Messrs. J. and C. H. Smithson who have met the promoters of the scheme in a most generous spirit.' The *Echo* seems to have all the details, including the 'reasonable' proposed purchase price, of a matter that was 'private and confidential' in the clerk to the Council's letter to Newton Brooke a week earlier.

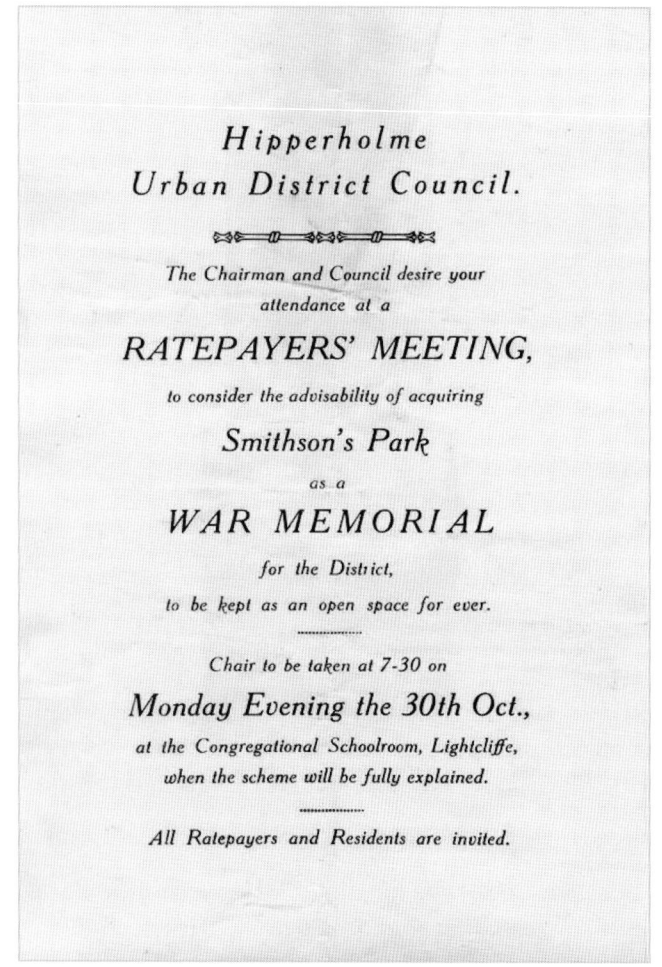

(Chris Helme Collection)

Ratepayers' Meeting

The meeting had been advertised as taking place on Monday, 30th October, yet the *Echo* reports that there was a 'large attendance' in the Congregational schoolroom on Tuesday evening.[45] It was chaired by Algernon Denham, chairman of the Council, who was supported on the platform by several councillors and the authority's clerk, accountant, and surveyor. Denham began by relating the various memorial schemes which had been considered.

1.   Provision of club premises 'to be used for the purposes of the social welfare of ex-soldiers and sailors.' This was rejected because it was felt that it would not provide 'a lasting benefit'.

2.   A cenotaph. This 'did not meet with general approval.' (There is no record in council minutes of a suggested cenotaph.)

3.   Purchase of Smithson Park. The asking price was between £4,000 and £5,000. This, together with the cost of upkeep, was beyond what could be raised in Hipperholme.

4. The 'most favoured' idea was the footpath (Denham called it a 'natural park') from Leeds and Whitehall Road to Bailiff Bridge, which was within the means of Hipperholme ratepayers. However, 'from lack of support and other difficulties, it finally fell to the ground.' There is no indication as to what the 'other difficulties' were, nor is there any reference to the proposed recreation ground 'near tunnel' which had been the subject of negotiations, and eventual agreement, between Joseph Walsh, on behalf of the war memorial committee, and Newton Brooke.

Having delivered his summary, the chairman said they were all present 'to start *de novo* with new propositions.' Negotiations with Charles and Joseph Smithson had continued and the brothers had now agreed to accept a much reduced price of £2,000. (It was later confirmed that Denham and Francis Horner, the clerk, had negotiated on the Council's behalf, had 'taken the initiative'.[46]) The Smithson brothers were referred to as 'those public-spirited gentlemen of Halifax' and were thanked for 'the generous manner in which they had treated the promoters of the scheme.' There was 'applause'. Denham said that he was frequently asked what Hipperholme had done to commemorate those who had given their lives in the war, when 'some 300 went out to serve their country, and about 70 had made the supreme sacrifice.' He had had to reply, "As yet we have done nothing." He hoped that 'after the vote had been taken that night … they would be enabled to say that no place had risen more unanimously and generously to the occasion than Hipperholme.' (More 'applause'.) On the subject of cost, the council's surveyor had estimated it would be no more than a penny (worth 42% of its decimalised namesake) on the rates. The gathering was reminded that the rates in Hipperholme were considerably lower than in all surrounding authorities.

Councillor Robinson agreed with the provision of a memorial but wondered what the cost of upkeep might be. He felt that Smithson Park was badly drained, which could prove a future financial burden if they decided to go ahead. Further, he questioned the need for another park in the district when there were already two (presumably George V and Bailiff Bridge). He felt that the west ward, which he represented, had been 'grossly neglected in the past', and that there were several alternative sites for a 'simple playing field'. However, he added that if the meeting passed the scheme, he would subscribe. Denham agreed that there was a need for a recreation ground in the ward Councillor Robinson represented, 'but this was a scheme for the whole of the district and not for one ward – (applause). He (the Chairman) had received 700 promises from the people of Bailiffe Bridge – (applause). He asked them not to look at the scheme in a narrow way.' (The list of subscribers, shown below, has 135 names, from the whole of the district. Perhaps Councillor Denham was referring to promises of support.)

The vicar of Coley, Dr. G. T. Jowett, wondered if Smithson Park was the most suitable location for a recreation ground. The offer was 'splendid' but perhaps there was a greater need in the west ward, where children had to play in the streets, 'having nowhere else to go.' Councillor Lumb responded that they welcomed criticism, 'but where in the district could they find a better or more commodious or suitable site for the purpose than the one offered to them?'[47] He thought it would be 'a great pity if the opportunity for the bargain was not clinched from that meeting.' This was met with 'applause'.

There were other speakers. Councillor Herbert Womersley 'spoke strongly in support. He was absolutely a Socialist and that was why he agreed to the public authority acquiring all the land possible that was cheap.'[48] Councillors Holgate and Wood were in favour, as was Mr. Fred Pohlmann, but a Mr. Brown 'criticised the scheme, observing that Smithson's Park was unsuitable.' Councillor Tom Holgate responded that 'in addition to part of the estate being drained, it was sheltered and would be warm and quite suitable for the purposes which the promoters of the scheme intended.'[49] The chairman would provide a list of subscribers and said that £2,450 had been promised, which does support the view that people had been donating to a fund for some time, rather than having a specific project in mind. But who knows what happens between the lines of council minutes and local newspaper reports? (You will observe that Newton Brooke increased his promise to £105, which places him higher on the list than the five who contributed £100.)

Councillor Denham concluded by proposing 'That the ratepayers of Hipperholme consider it advisable to acquire Smithson's estate for the people of Hipperholme.' Fred Pohlmann seconded. The proposal was carried unanimously.

COUNCIL OFFICES,
HIPPERHOLME.

17th November, 1922.

Dear Sir or Madam,

HIPPERHOLME URBAN DISTRICT WAR MEMORIAL.

As you may be aware, it has been decided to acquire the estate known as Smithson's Park as a War Memorial for the District. It is proposed that the property should be known as "The Memorial Stray" and laid out somewhat on the lines of the Harrogate "Stray," with intersecting paths, and that a Memorial suitably inscribed should be erected in some convenient position.

The proposal has received enthusiastic support and a magnificent start has been made in the collection of the money required. The Committee feel that, whether the scheme be regarded as a War Memorial or as an open space, every resident, both rich and poor, will welcome the opportunity of contributing something, according to his or her means as a thanksgiving offering, and for the welfare of the District.

The Hipperholme District is one of the few areas in the West Riding without a War Memorial, and the Committee are of opinion that every resident will be anxious to be rid of that unenviable distinction.

It is desirable in every way that a further £1,000 should be raised without delay, and the Committee urge you to give the matter your earnest consideration in order that you may be prepared to inform the canvasser who will call upon you some time between the 20th and 30th November what you are prepared to contribute. We are instructed to enclose you herewith a list of donations to date, together with a contribution slip, the filling in of which will materially lighten the labours of the voluntary workers who have undertaken the task of a house-to-house collection.

The Memorial is a District Memorial, and we confidently appeal to every resident to contribute something, no matter how small, towards it.

On behalf of the Committee,

We are, Yours faithfully,

A. Denham. Chairman.

Francis M. Holmes. Secretary.

John E. Barker. Treasurer.

Following the decision, matters moved rapidly. The *Echo* of 10th November, only eleven days later, reports that £2834.1s.0d. has been raised, from a total of 132 people. (This is the equivalent of more than £200,000 in today's money.) Nevertheless, Algernon Denham and his council appealed, a week later, for contributions from 'every resident … no matter how small'.

(This letter, and the List of Promised Donations on the opposite page, are from the Chris Helme Collection.)

HIPPERHOLME WAR MEMORIAL.

LIST OF PROMISED DONATIONS.

	£	s.	d.
Sir W. H. Aykroyd	200	0	0
R. Lumb and Family	150	0	0
N. Brooke	105	0	0
A. Denham	100	0	0
Anonymous	100	0	0
R. H. Goldthorpe	100	0	0
F. & C. Smithson	100	0	0
Sir J. W. Bulmer	100	0	0
Mrs. W. C. Womersley and Family	52	10	0
W. Glossop	52	10	0
F. M. Horner	50	0	0
N. Wood	50	0	0
F. Pohlmann	50	0	0
E. Bottomley	50	0	0
J. H. Fletcher	50	0	0
Anonymous	50	0	0
E. B. Osborne	50	0	0
W. Sucksmith	50	0	0
B. Casson	50	0	0
W. Barraclough	50	0	0
T. H. Walker	50	0	0
W. W. Milnes	50	0	0
C. E. Dickinson	50	0	0
C. Robinson	50	0	0
G. S. Haslam	50	0	0
Mr. and Mrs. C. Hanson	50	0	0
S. Watkinson Junr.	50	0	0
B. O. Osborne	50	0	0
Harry Pickles	50	0	0
J. Pearson	50	0	0
Dr. F. C. Mills	30	0	0
A. Sharpe	25	0	0
C. E. Rose	25	0	0
H. M. Horner	25	0	0
T. Wayman	25	0	0
W. Bussey	25	0	0
T. H. Hartley	25	0	0
Anonymous	25	0	0
H. Whittaker	25	0	0
D. S. Greenwood	25	0	0
J. Pickles	25	0	0
J. Hill	20	0	0
W. H. Foster	20	0	0
E. J. Reddie	20	0	0
Mrs. Hind	20	0	0
A. H. Wright	20	0	0
J. H. Knowles	10	10	0
Mr. and Mrs. Ackroyd	10	10	0
Stocks Brewery Co.	10	10	0
T. Holgate	10	0	0
F. H. Brown	10	0	0
E. Read	10	0	0
Mrs. Bateman	10	0	0
W. W. Longbottom	10	0	0
R. Sugden	10	0	0
H. Gough	10	0	0
J. Clay	10	0	0
E. W. Norris	5	0	0
A. Butterfield	5	0	0
J. Lawson	5	0	0
Rev. H. L. Taylor	5	0	0
G. Webster & Son, Ltd.	5	0	0
G. Moorhouse	5	0	0
J. Hebblethwaite	5	0	0
H. Womersley	5	0	0
J. Oates	5	0	0
A. V. Sutcliffe	5	0	0
T. Wressell	5	0	0
W. H. Naylor	5	0	0
J. Brooke	5	0	0
G. Hey	5	0	0
Mrs. E. J. Reddie	5	0	0
Mrs. H. L. Taylor	5	0	0
Mrs. A. Denham	5	0	0
J. Denham	5	0	0
Mrs. C. E. Rose	5	0	0
Mrs. W. Sucksmith	5	0	0
R. Ainley	5	0	0
S. Dean	5	0	0
J. E. Barker	5	0	0
J. Sykes	5	0	0
Mrs. J. Sykes	5	0	0
Mr. and Mrs. W. Bottomley	5	0	0
A. Aspinall	5	0	0
Mr. and Mrs. Pearson	5	0	0
Mrs. A. H. Wright	5	0	0
J. Firth	5	0	0
Mrs. N. Wood	5	0	0
J. Kemp	5	0	0
G. Haigh	5	0	0
T. Kemp	5	0	0
J. W. Holmes	5	0	0
L. Wood	5	0	0
Anonymous	5	0	0
E. H. Naylor	5	0	0
F. Smith	5	0	0
J. K. Shepley	5	0	0
H. Coates	5	0	0
Mr. and Mrs. J. Stevens	5	0	0
S. Sunderland	5	0	0
J. Sunderland	5	0	0
H. and N. Armitage	5	0	0
C. Barraclough	5	0	0
Mrs. C. Barraclough	5	0	0
G. Webster & Sons. (2nd. donation)	5	0	0
A. V. Naylor	5	0	0
S. M. Sutcliffe	5	0	0
G. Wheeler	3	3	0
Miss Fitton	2	10	0
Miss Broadbent	2	10	0
H. Dyson	2	2	0
E. Illingworth	2	2	0
Mrs. T. Holgate	2	0	0
E. Laycock	1	1	0
Mr. and Mrs. F. Lee	1	1	0
Mrs. Hague	1	1	0
G. G. Hague	1	1	0
E. Rodgers	1	0	0
Miss McKie	1	0	0
Miss Mackintosh	1	0	0
F. J. Harris	1	0	0
Mr. Houseman	1	0	0
W. Ascroft	1	0	0
Mr. Andrews	1	0	0
Mrs. Lindley	1	0	0
Mrs. Carr	1	0	0
F. Wilkinson	1	0	0
H. C. Carmichael	1	0	0
Mr. and Mrs. Bowes	1	0	0
G. T. Reynolds		10	0
S. Turner		10	0
J. W. Hickman		10	0
A. Schofield		10	0
A. B. Wakefield		10	0
Mrs. F. E. Wakefield		10	0
	2834	1	0

Sub-committees

On the following Tuesday a meeting of subscribers, held at the council offices, was 'well attended'. The clerk, Francis Horner, set out their aims, adding that, whatever suggestions were made as to the 'laying-out' of the park should be unanimous. If anyone held a minority view, they should 'drop it and join in with those in the majority.' Algernon Denham was unanimously voted to chair the meeting. He repeated what he had said the previous week regarding price and the amount already subscribed, adding that he 'did not think there was another district in England of the size of Hipperholme that had done so splendid [sic].' In addition to Denham, officials were to be Horner as secretary, and the Council's accountant, J. E. Barker, as treasurer. A committee of twenty-seven was appointed 'to get out schemes of the "lay out", rules and regulations, and submit the same to a general meeting of subscribers for final approval.' A list of the members is of interest.

> 'Messrs, J. F. Walsh, W.W. Longbottom, F. Farrar and S. Dean (local architects), Lady Aykroyd, Mrs. H. L. Taylor, Mrs. Bussey, Mrs. T. Wayman, Mrs. C. E. Dickinson, Mrs. Wood, Couns. T. Holgate, R. Lumb, C. Robinson, N. Wood, H. Womersley, J.P., Messrs. B. O. Osborne, C. E. Rose, E. J. Reddie, F. Pohlmann, W. H. Foster, R. Ainley, W. Barraclough, G. G. Hague, J. Kemp, W. Sucksmith, W. W. Milnes and C. E. Dickinson.'

This assembly of prominent local citizens included, in addition to councillors and council officials, the heads of Lightcliffe National Schools and Hipperholme Grammar School (Hague and Kemp) and the vicar's wife (Mrs. Taylor); also the captain of Lightcliffe cricket club's first team (Foster). The other individuals were also influential in village concerns of the day.

Much time at this gathering seems to have been given over to debate about a delicate matter relating to 'Hipperholme and Lightcliffe Tennis Club.' During a discussion on another topic with Councillor Wood, Denham discovered that the club was having to leave its premises and, in apparent ignorance of developing plans for Smithson Park, had made a move in the hope of acquiring some of the land for their club. Wood was a member of the club and, as such, was intending to pursue this request with the Smithson family. (It seems unlikely that Councillor Wood would be unaware of plans for the park, but perhaps, as suggested in Horner's letter of 20th October to Newton Brooke, plans really were 'private and confidential', known only to the two negotiators, Denham and Horner). Denham felt, in the circumstances, there was 'a moral obligation ... as well as a legal one' owing to the club. He wished to see that 'fair play was done', although he does seem to have second thoughts when he reiterates that the committee's scheme was for the benefit of the whole community. He has 'no axe to grind', adding enigmatically that 'Some of his strongest critics belonged to the club.' The dilemma is 'discussed at some length', before a decision is made that 'the moral obligations which had been referred to by the chairman should be adhered to if the tennis club wished.'

It is difficult to understand fully the nature of this 'moral obligation'. If Denham and Horner had negotiated with the Smithson brothers in ignorance of the approaches of the tennis club, they hadn't been acting in an underhand manner. On the other hand, surely the Smithsons would be aware of the tennis club's interest, in which case why were the Council negotiators not acquainted with the alternative interest in what can only have been a small portion of the land in question? Perhaps the dilemma arose because of the personalities involved. In a small village a hundred years ago it is unlikely those involved would be unknown to each other. However, there is no doubt it was a 'dilemma', as a later meeting would reveal.

A fortnight later the war memorial committee met. I take this to be the group which was constituted in July 1919 (see p.27) rather than the newly convened organisation. Councillor Denham was still in the chair, however. Hipperholme urban district 'was divided into 16 areas, and a collector appointed to be responsible for each portion.' Also, a further sub-committee was formed, 'to consider the layout of Smithson's Estate, and submit a report to the next meeting'. A fortnight earlier the subscribers' committee had been given the same brief regarding the design of the park. Four original members of the war memorial committee – Councillors Denham, Walsh, Lumb and Herbert Womersley – were also part of the larger organisation.

Trouble at Bailiff Bridge

Bailiff Bridge already had a memorial, yet they were being asked to contribute, through future payment of rates, to the cost of another, and one situated a mile up the road in Lightcliffe; indeed, almost in Hipperholme. Of course, they hadn't financed their cenotaph and small park, but it was obviously felt there was a need to placate the villagers. To that end, 'to enlist sympathy', a meeting of ratepayers and other residents was held at the Oddfellows Hall on Tuesday 28th November.[50] After a delay of years, no time was being wasted.

The attendance was 'not very large' as Ernest B. Osborn took the chair, supported by Councillors Denham and Aspinall and officers Barker and Dean, accountant and surveyor.[51] At the request of the chairman, Denham explained the scheme. He enumerated and described the four options which had been investigated, as he had done at the Lightcliffe Congregational church a month earlier. He also repeated that the rates in the Hipperholme U.D.C. were lower than any around, and mentioned the 'moral obligation' to the Lightcliffe tennis club. Denham regarded the purchase of Smithson Park as 'the finest thing they could do'. It was a project for the whole district and, 'Bailiffe Bridge being a portion of the district, they ought to have their say in the matter.' Thanks to Sir William Aykroyd and Sir Algernon Firth they had their 'magnificent Memorial and Garden', but he was confident that they would 'desire benefit' (odd choice of words) from the scheme. The members of the Council had subscribed between £500 and £600 to the appeal because 'they recognised better than anyone else what a benefit it would be to future generations.' (When the Stray was opened the following September, the *Echo* account referred to the residents of Hipperholme and Lightcliffe, and the procession included the children of St. Matthew's and Lightcliffe Congregational churches and Hipperholme Wesleyan chapel. No mention of Bailiff Bridge.)

The need to justify the inevitable increase in rates was the purpose of the meeting, and the plausibility of Denham's rationale began to suffer. They were 'only asking the ratepayers to give so much in the pound of that which the members of the Council had saved them in the past.' Furthermore, 'If additional houses were built on the Leeds and Whitehall Road, and the estate being an open space would be an incentive towards this, he felt sure that the rates from the houses would pay for the upkeep of the "Stray"... He knew of no place which, during the time of stress and strife, had come out better than Bailiffe Bridge, and one reason for that was that the Council had kept the rates down, and he had the authority of Sir William Aykroyd for saying that.' (A smart tactic, to invoke the support of the village's chief employer.) Denham concluded with the assertion that 'their children's children would feel proud that the people of Bailiffe Bridge in 1922 had been connected with one of the finest schemes that had ever been introduced into Hipperholme.' There was 'applause' for this fine rhetorician, followed by questions from the floor.

Why was there no recreation ground at Bailiff Bridge, especially as there had been a collection at the coronation (of George V in 1911) for the purchase of the field where the memorial garden now stood, specifically for that purpose? The questioners were assured that the land had been purchased by Sir William Aykroyd from Ripley's trustees. Mr. J. T. Pearson wanted to know why they had not been consulted earlier. Denham replied that 'a public meeting was called by advertisement and held in the most central place in the district [Lightcliffe Congregational church] … Seeing that there were not many people from Bailiffe Bridge at the first meeting, they had come down that night to give the residents all information and to enlist their sympathy.' Mr. Pearson commented that people in the village felt they had not been consulted, though he did say that he supported the scheme. There was further support from three other gentlemen, before the chairman, Mr. Osborn, made a final appeal.

He recalled how the villagers had sent out food parcels during the war, and how welcome those were to the soldiers, himself included. What was being proposed was a lasting memorial to those who had fallen, and he 'felt certain that Bailiffe Bridge would not be behind in assisting the district to show their high appreciation of what the lads had done'. There was more applause, after which the Bailiffe Bridge Soldiers' and Sailors' Committee agreed to see that the village was canvassed for subscriptions.

'Interesting Scheme Nearing Fruition'

The *Halifax Courier* of 15 February 1923 reported a meeting of subscribers to the Hipperholme War Memorial Fund, held the previous evening at the Congregational church schoolroom. There was an attendance of 120 which, as the number of subscribers was 135, indicates the importance to the community of the proposed memorial park.

Councillor Denham took the chair, saying the object of the meeting was to put before subscribers the 'arrangements provisionally made by the committee'. He said that the committee numbered twenty-five (two of the original twenty-seven must have left) and that their meetings had regularly been attended by 'well over 20'. £3,627 had been raised, which was 'far beyond the most optimistic expectations … No other district had been so successful.' Smithson's Park would cost £2,000. 'Additional purchases had been provisionally arranged with Messrs. Naylor and Baines for plots of land adjoining, and also two exchanges had been concluded with Mr. Osborne and Mr. Rose.'[52] These exchanges had enhanced the scheme and the 'very generous spirit' of the four gentlemen was commended. 'The committee suggested that this park should be designated "The Memorial Stray".' It was possible, Denham continued, that the eventual cost would exceed the estimate, in which case there were 'other sources of income to tap if it were found necessary.' The layout had been designed by four local architects, including Mr. Dean, the council's surveyor. (The others, as we have seen, were Walsh, Longbottom and Farrar.) If there were sufficient funds it was intended to provide a shelter, and there would be the opportunity for people to supply additional seats. Finally, the transfer of this property 'had been made to Mr. E. J. Reddie, Mr. F. Pohlmann, and Mr. A. Denham. As was well known, on completion, the Stray would be handed over to the District Council, who would defray the cost of upkeep from the public funds.'[53]

Francis Horner, the clerk, summarised the conditions attached to the use of the Stray.

1. It shall be an open space for ever, used as a public park and for no other purpose.

2. No buildings shall be erected other than those incidental to the scheme.

3. Admittance to the Stray shall be free of charge, except that six days in each year shall be reserved at the discretion of the Council, and the net revenue from those days shall be used for the benefit of the Stray.

4. All expense of upkeep, etc., shall be paid out of public funds.

5. Bylaws will be issued by the Council, but these will be framed to meet the wishes of the subscribers as far as possible.

Mr. Longbottom explained the layout in detail, saying that a 'suitable memorial would be placed in a conspicuous position'.

The following resolution was then put to the meeting:

> 'That this meeting of subscribers to the memorial fund hereby confirm the purchase of lands from Messrs. Smithson, Baines and Naylor, and the exchanges of lands with Messrs. Osborn and Rose, and hereby adopt the plan of the lay-out, and the memorial as submitted and recommended by the committee.'

The resolution was proposed by Councillor Denham and seconded by Councillor Holgate. It was carried unanimously. 'In reply to questions it was stated that the right of public meetings or any public demonstration would not be allowed on the Stray, neither could it be used for any political purpose whatsoever.'

The *Halifax Courier* deals briefly with the Lightcliffe tennis club 'moral obligation' referred to above; the *Echo* gives the clearly contentious matter more detail.[54] In his opening address Denham had asked the meeting to 'eliminate … from their minds for the moment' both this matter and the application from Councillor Wood to purchase a portion of Smithson Park. (This is the first reference to Councillor Wood wishing to make a purchase as a private individual, rather than as an officer of the tennis club.)

Councillor Wood was also negotiating on behalf of the tennis club. Denham repeated what he had assured Wood: that if the land were acquired by the Council, 'he would do his utmost to get the Tennis Club housed on the Stray.' There was a 'long and heated discussion'. Councillor Holgate 'stated that, from information he had received, Messrs. Smithson would not have sold a portion of the land separately and consequently the Tennis Club could not have purchased any land there.' (If this was the case, why could the Smithsons have not made this clear, thus eliminating any question of a 'moral obligation'?) Councillor H. Womersley responded that Holgate's point was irrelevant; all they should be concerned with was whether they had an honourable obligation to the club, 'and so long as he remained in public life he would take his stand for doing the only right and reasonable thing.' He also 'twitted' Holgate for originally supporting the tennis club, only to change his stance when he realised the tendency of public opinion.[55]

The motion was that the portion of land be sold to the tennis club. The voting could not have been closer. The *Courier* says that it was 45 to 47, the *Echo* 'a single vote', 45 to 46. Either way, there were almost thirty abstentions. The tennis club would not have new courts on Smithson Park. There may be no connection, but when Aykroyd was awarded his baronetcy in 1920, the *Echo* said, in summarising his life, that 'his was the hand which greatly assisted the villagers of Lightcliffe in the laying-out of their cricket field, and now he and Sir Algernon [Firth] are furthering the social benefits of the district by bearing the cost of the new tennis club which is being formed in connection with the Lightcliffe Cricket Club.' At the opening of the new pavilion in July 1922, the club had been referred to as 'Lightcliffe Cricket and Lawn Tennis Club'. The president of the cricket club was Councillor Algernon Denham. The tennis club flourished there for more than fifty years.

Algernon Denham addresses the audience at the opening of the new Lightcliffe Cricket Club pavilion in 1923. Seated to his right, holding the notes for his speech, is William Womersley. Two chairmen of Hipperholme U.D.C., and of Lightcliffe C.C.

The separate request from Councillor Wood to purchase 480 square yards of Smithson Park also gave rise to a 'lengthy discussion'. It was decided (no details as to voting) that 'no part of the land be sold to Cllr. Wood.' However, there are a couple of confusing sentences in the *Echo*.

> 'It appeared that Coun. Wood was a sub-tenant of Coun. Holgate, while there were also other tenants on the estate. Messrs. Smithson's [sic], it appears, gave some of the occupiers an option to purchase but forgot Coun. Wood, and later expressed a wish that the latter should not be allowed to suffer by what had been an oversight.'

Tom Holgate (*left, courtesy of John Illingworth*) was a local farmer and milkman, who, as already mentioned, grazed his cows on Smithson Park.

(The photograph, taken on Till Carr Lane, dates from an earlier time when Holgate lived at Till Carr Farm.)

It seems Holgate sub-let a small portion of the land he rented to his council colleague. Who were the other tenants? Were these the people who built houses on the west side of Sutherland Road, or those who built the semi-detached Netherfield and Rylstone on Wakefield Road, soon to be surrounded on two sides by a public park?

Summary

Hipperholme Urban District Council was to have its memorial and its park. Looking back from the perspective of a century this seems to have taken longer than should have been necessary, and there are aspects of the process which are puzzling. Why did the memorial walk / recreation ground idea, so enthusiastically promoted during the later months of 1919 until early February 1920, disappear without trace, to be quickly replaced, within less than a month, by the Smithson Park scheme? Why did it then take two-and-a-half years for the progress of this scheme to be made public? There had been fundraising for some three years by then, as evidenced by Newton Brooke's reference, when, in January 1920, he offered to subscribe £100 to the 'Memorial Fund'. The upper case initial letters would appear to confirm the existence of a formal arrangement, corroborated by the appearance of an initial list of 101 names in the *Brighouse Echo*.

Algernon Denham, chairman of the Council, and Francis Horner, the clerk, had negotiated with the Smithson brothers. The initial asking price was '£4-5,000', but was considerably reduced to £2,000. We are told this was due to the 'generous spirit' of the brothers. Why was this spirit initially lacking, when the idea for the use of the land must have been clear from the outset? Or perhaps it was suggested to the brothers that the drainage problem rendered that land unsuitable for any other purpose. (Remember Joan Ing and Sour Ing.) The scheme was in place by the time of the October meeting. Why were the details 'private and confidential' in correspondence between Horner and Brooke, yet days later were released in full to the *Brighouse Echo*? Brooke is not mentioned again after the exchange of letters prior to the meeting. What was his involvement?

Algernon Denham was central to the negotiations, the ratepayers' meeting, and the subsequent public relations exercise with the residents of Bailiff Bridge. Why, at the meeting, was there no mention of the recreation ground at Hipperholme, when a price had been agreed between Joseph Walsh and Brooke? What were the 'other difficulties' which curtailed enthusiasm for the walk / recreation ground idea? Why is there no reference, in council minutes or local newspapers, to a cenotaph idea, referred to by Denham at the meeting? Finally, the apparent importance of the 'moral obligation' to the tennis club is odd. If the club was merely considering making an offer for a portion of Smithson Park, why was there such an obligation? There is no confirmation that an offer had already been made. Denham supported the tennis club to the extent that, when the 'moral obligation' was overturned, its members were presumably accommodated as part of the new tennis section at Lightcliffe Cricket Club, of which Denham was president.

However, all this might be no more than the unfounded imaginings of a mind alert for political deviousness. The overwhelming outcome of the negotiations, open or secret, would be a fitting and lasting memorial to the 110 villagers of Hipperholme, Lightcliffe and Bailiff Bridge who had lost their young lives due to 'the war that was called Great',[56] and hopefully some comfort for the community in its collective grief. The generations of those who came after and grew up around the Stray could not have been more grateful.

CHAPTER 5

OPENING CEREMONY

KATHLEEN HEATON was eight years old in 1923. She lived with her family on Park View, 'under the lidgate'. As Kathleen Briggs, of Knowle Top Drive, she spoke to the Lightcliffe & District Local History Society in 1998 about her childhood in the village. One of her recollections was of being taken by her father, on the evening of 8 September 1923, to watch the granite plinth on the Stray memorial being lowered into place under the illumination of arc lights. The 'Memorial Stray' was opened the following day, so the organisers were cutting it fine. The unveiling was preceded by a procession of ex-servicemen and Sunday school scholars and teachers, headed by the Band of the First 4th West Riding Regiment, from the council offices to the memorial.

Preparations. Benches in place, union flag draped around the memorial. You can see the banked-up earth around the memorial. Contrast this with photographs in the coming chapters of flourishing flower beds and hedges, the area transformed in a few years.   *(John Illingworth Collection)*

Attended by 'two or three thousand', held in 'ideal weather', the event was reported in detail in the *Brighouse Echo* of the following Friday. I can do no better than reproduce the newspaper's splendid account of the event, with the addition of a few illustrations, only one of which was included in the article.

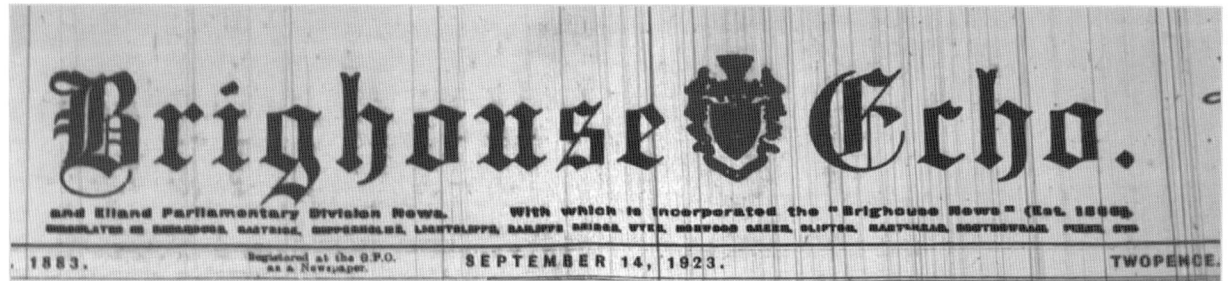

Brighouse Echo.

and Elland Parliamentary Division News.   With which is incorporated the "Brighouse News" (Est. 1869).

1883.   Registered at the G.P.O. as a Newspaper.   SEPTEMBER 14, 1923.   TWOPENCE.

The HIPPERHOLME "STRAY."

UNIQUE WAR MEMORIAL.

TRIBUTE TO FALLEN HEROES.

IMPRESSIVE PUBLIC CEREMONIAL.

UNVEILING, DEDICATION AND TREE PLANTING.

A war memorial of an unusual character, if not indeed unique in form, was inaugurated at Hipperholme on Sunday last. The scheme has been in progress for about 12 months, its inspiration having come from Councillor Algernon Denham, J.P., chairman of the District Council, and Mr F. M. Horner, the Clerk, who found little difficulty in securing the necessary co-operation of Messrs. C. H. and J. H. Smithson, who sold a portion of their estates on generous terms, and also a good number of subscribers and voluntary workers in carrying out a project of such an important interesting character. The idea was that the War Memorial of the district should consist, in the main, of a large open space, to be known as The Stray, and modelled somewhat on the lines of the famous Stray in Harrogate, in which should be placed a special cenotaph to record the memory of those who laid down their lives during the late war and the gratitude of the residents of the township to all who served with the colours. This purpose has been admirably achieved, and the thousands of spectators who attended the ceremony of last Sunday afternoon will warm in their congratulations to all concerned.

Full descriptions of the details of the scheme have already been given, but it is worth recalling that the Stray consists of 12½ acres of parkland, which has been acquired by a committee of influential townspeople as to 12 acres from Messrs. Joseph and Chas. Smithson. The remaining land was acquired from the executors of Mr. Naylor, late of Lydgate House, and the executors of Mrs. Baines. The contour of the estate has also been considerably improved by small exchanges of land with Mr. Osborne and Mr. Rose. The memorial itself is a handsome structure and has cost between £700 and £800. Mr. W. W. Longbottom, F.R.I.B.A., who is a member of the Memorial Committee, has officiated as hon. architect, and has designed the cenotaph, which is a fitting tribute to the memory of the fallen. The monument erected on the memorial Stray is placed on the rising ground abutting upon the Leeds and Whitehall Road, so it commands an outlook over the whole of the spacious grounds. The design has been prepared specially to suit this selected site, to obtain the best effect architecturally, and also with the object of providing sheltered seating accommodation having a south aspect.

Waiting for proceedings to begin (left)
(Chris Helme Collection)

The plan of the structure is semi-circular. In the centre rises the principal feature, consisting of a substantially erected stone base supporting a single column of Shap granite, 14ft. high, roughly shaped as an obelisk, and weighing about 8 tonnes. On each side of this central feature, the curved retaining walls form the seat enclosure. These walls are augmented by suitably designed railings. At the outer ends of the semi-circular walls are placed flights of stone steps leading to an upper terrace, so that while the front of the memorial overlooks the Stray, showing the full height of 30ft., the opposite side, facing the main road, shows 23ft high. On the front overlooking the Stray is inserted a plain Aberdeen granite cross. On the side facing Leeds Road is placed a bronze tablet with the incised lettering, filled with cream enamel, bearing the inscription:-

"This memorial was erected and this Stray dedicated to the public forever, in remembrance of those residents who gave their lives, and in gratitude to those survivors who gave their services in the European War, 1914-18."

The total cost of the War Memorial has been well over £4,000, and previous to last weekend about £ 3,800 had been received in subscriptions, so that it is not anticipated any difficulty will be experienced in defraying the expense which the handsome and comprehensive scheme has involved. A sum of £68 14s. was received from the collection and sale of programmes. Coun. Denham has been chairman of the committee and Mr F. M. Horner, Clerk to the District Council, has acted as hon. secretary.

THE DEDICATION CEREMONY.

The notable event was favoured by gloriously fine weather, and there was an assembly of several thousand spectators at the unveiling and dedication ceremony, which was appropriately associated with due religious observances, last Sunday afternoon. Most of the leading residents of the Hipperholme and Lightcliffe districts were present, as well as many distinguished visitors from neighbouring towns, and for these seats were provided on the space behind the memorial stones, besides the relatives of some 70 men who laid down their lives. The children from the Sunday Schools of St. Matthew's Church, Lightcliffe Congregational Church, and Hipperholme Wesleyan Chapel, marched in procession, and a very large company of ex-servicemen, commanded by Coun. C. Robinson was headed by the band of the 4th West Riding Regiment. Excellent service was rendered by the local police, under Inspector Wood, and the local special constables also helped in the maintenance of order, their chief responsibilities consisting of the direction of invited guests and others to the place is appointed for them.

The unveiling ceremony was conducted by the Rt. Hon. J. H. Whitley, M.P. for Halifax, Speaker of the House of Commons, and the dedication was by the Rt. Rev. Bishop Frodsham, D.D., vicar of Halifax.[57] Others taking part in the service work the Rev. H. L. Taylor (vicar of Lightcliffe), Rev. J. H. N. Tomsen (curate),[58] Rev. A. J. Farnsworth (Hipperholme Wesleyan Church), and Rev. Hugh Jenkins, M.A. (Batley). Amongst others in the large assembly were Mr Joseph H. Smithson, J.P., and Mrs Smithson, Mr. C. H. Smithson, J.P., and Mrs Smithson, Miss Phyllis Whitley (daughter of the Speaker), Mrs Frodsham, Coun. A. Denham, J.P., and Mrs Denham, Alderman and Mrs. G. F. Sugden (Mayor of Brighouse), Mr. P. T. Grove (Town Clerk of Brighouse), Colonel and Mrs. R. E. Sugden, Mr C. Ramsden J.P., and Mrs Ramsden (Halifax), Dr. G. T. Jowett (vicar of Coley), Mr. John Lister, Mr. A. B. Wakefield, Mrs. Wakefield, J.P., Mrs. R. Lumb, Major H. H. Aykroyd, Major E. P. Chambers, Captain W. Winterburn, Mr. E. Armitage, Mr. Jonas Crabtree, Mr. J. B. Carter, J.P., Mr. W. W. Longbottom, Coun. N. Wood, Coun. E. Bottomley, Coun. T. Holgate, Coun. G. Hey, Mr. F. M. Horner, Mr. S. Dean (surveyor), and Mr S. Ashcroft (accountant).

The service of unveiling and dedication was of the simplest possible character, commencing with the hymn "Oh God, our help in ages past." This was sung by the entire company, an excellent lead being given by the combined choirs of the local churches, and the band accompanying. Alternately bandmaster A. Higgins and Mr. L. Ambler, A.R.C.O., officiated as conductor, the latter taking charge of the unaccompanied singing. The Vicar of Lightcliffe led short prayers and the 23rd Psalm was chanted, the Rev. A. J. Farnsworth reading the lesson from Ecclesiastes 44 – "Let us now praise famous men," etc.

The Rt. Hon. J. H. Whitley, in the midst of intense silence, then delivered a brief but singularly apposite address, moving in its terms and delivered with clarity and impressiveness of tone and gesture. "Fellow citizens,' said the speaker, in his opening remarks, 'meditation is better than speech on an occasion such as this. Words other than those of praise or prayer should be few. It is a time of remembrance and dedication. You have raised these stones of remembrance so that those who come after may never forget a great story of sacrifice and devotion. The men whose names you record upon them were of us and like us. We did not know their qualities until the great call came. From the field or the workshop, from the school or the university they came, young citizens, brave cheery determined, ready to give all for the inheritance of liberty won for them by those who have gone before. This memorial should be more than a record of our reverence for those who have died and our gratitude to those who served. It should carry a message through long future years to those of other generations who may pass by. Instead of speech I have searched for a few simple words which might be written in your hearts, and perhaps taught to your boys. They might be a meditation when we bow our heads before these stones. They were written by a living poet, Henry Newbolt, for a memorial to his schoolfellows:-

"Praise God for these,
and pray their like to be;
they saved the world,
yet here they lived as we."

The Ceremony, showing the huge community interest in the opening of the Hipperholme and Lightcliffe Memorial Stray. This photograph was in the Brighouse Echo of 14 September 1923.

The Speaker of the House pulled the cord which released the Union Jack with which the obelisk was covered, and the military stood to attention. The hymn, "O, valiant hearts, who to your glory came," was sung, after which Bishop Frodsham dedicated the memorial with the following words:-

> 'In the faith of Jesus Christ I do now dedicate this Memorial to the glory of God and in memory of all those belonging to this township who laid down their lives and in gratitude to those survivors who gave their services for God, King and country during the Great War, in the name of the Father and of the Son and of the Holy Ghost.'

The Rev Hugh Jenkins led the concluding prayers, which were followed by the hymn "For all the Saints who from their labours rest." The Bishop pronounced the blessing, the pathetic notes of the "Last Post" and the ringing challenge of the "Reveille" were sounded and the National Anthem closed this portion of the ceremony.

This could be Bishop Frodsham (to the right of the plinth) dedicating the memorial,
after J. H. Whitley has pulled the cord which released the union flag.

FLORAL OFFERINGS.

A very large number of relatives and friends of departed soldiers placed floral tributes of love at the foot of the memorial. There were beautiful baskets of flowers, many wreaths and crosses, and simple bunches from the home gardens, and all were equally touching in their sentiment and intention. Many bore cards with suitable inscriptions; none but those who brought them knew from whom others came; but they all gave evidence of personal regard and memories that will never fade. Amongst the number were the following:

"To honour those to whom this memorial is erected," from members of the Memorial Committee.

"In everlasting gratitude to those who made the supreme sacrifice," from the ratepayers of the Urban District of Hipperholme.

"In memory of fallen comrades of all regiments," from the local Ex-Service Men.

"In memory of our dear brother and all the boys of the district who made the supreme sacrifice in the European war, 1914-1918," from Mr. and Mrs. A. Denham, Lower Crow Nest.

"In grateful remembrance," from Sir Wm. and Lady Aykroyd, Cliff Hill, Lightcliffe.

"In remembrance," from Mr. and Mrs. Alfred H. Aykroyd, Hargreaves Head, Northowram, and Mr Harold H. Aykroyd, Cliff Hill, Lightcliffe.

"Remembrance," from Mr. and Mrs. A. B. Wakefield, Sept.,9th, 1914. March 9th 1915.

"In memory of my old boys," from Mr. G. G. Hague, School House Lightcliffe.

"With deepest sympathy," from Mr. and Mrs. J. Sucksmith, Mr. and Mrs. J. Asquith, and Mr. and Mrs. D. Robertshaw.

"With deepest sympathy," from Mr. and Mrs. Sucksmith and family and Willie.

"In loving memory of my dear father, Cpl. Pugh," from Dorothy.

"In loving memory of Pte. Arthur Thoseby, reported missing October 23rd 1916," from his mother, father, sisters, brothers and grandma.

"In loving memory of our dear son," Pte. N. Kirkbright, killed in action, from his father, mother, and brother Ronald.

"In memory of our fallen lads. They died for right and liberty," from a soldier's mother.

"In loving memory of a dear brother, Pte. Kylatt Wakefield," from his dear little sister, Susie.

"In affectionate remembrance of our dear son and brother, Pte. Arthur Broadley, Hipperholme."

"In memory of those who fell," from two who served.

"In loving memory of our dear nephew, Pte. Herbert Schofield, no. 4,877 1/7th Gordon Highlanders," from his uncle and aunt, Mr. and Mrs. H. Briggs.

"In loving remembrance of our dear Roland, who was killed in action, December 9th 1915," from his mother, brother, and sisters, Grange Terrace.

"In loving memory of Sec. Lieut. Harold Hoyle, Loyal North Lancashire Regiment, killed in action, July 23rd 1916."

"In loving memory of Pte. James Smallwood, 2nd Battalion Grenadier Guards, who was killed in action July 31st 1917," from sisters and brothers, Roylands Farm.

"Love's renewed tribute to a dear son and brother, Pte. Kylatt Wakefield, reported missing April 11th, 1918. Time does not change our thoughts of him: love and sweet memories linger still," from his sorrowing father, mother, brothers and sisters.

"For King and Country. In ever loving memory of our dear son, Pte. Harry Spence, Machine Gun Corps, aged 17 years. Just a boy, but he answered his country's call and laid his richest gift on the altar of duty, his life. R.I.P."

"In loving memory of our dear Uncle Jim," from Joan and Peggy.

"In affectionate remembrance of Harold Sharp," from the Longlands, Lightcliffe.

"They also served who anxiously watched and prayed," D. and E. A. Thornton.

"In loving memory of our dear boy," Arnold Hemingway.

"In loving memory of a dear brother Pte. Kylatt Wakefield," from his little Eric.

From the scholars and teachers of the Lightcliffe Congregational Sunday School.

From the Primary Department, Lightcliffe Congregational Sunday School.

"In loving remembrance of a dear husband and father," from Mrs. W. H. Bailey and family.

"In memory of our dear son, Pte. Herbert Schofield. No. 4877 1/7th Gordon Highlanders. An unseen string in memories heart is softly touched today. A token of love," from his father, mother, brother and sisters."

MEMORIAL TREES.

To commemorate the occasion, trees were planted on the Stray, on each side of the main path below the memorial, these honours being accorded to Pte. Jim Sucksmith (representing the ex-servicemen of the district), the Rt. Hon. J. H. Whitley, Mr. C. H. Smithson, J. P., Mr. Joseph H. Smithson, J. P., and Mrs. Algernon Denham. The work of tree planting was supervised by Messrs. S. Dean and Hemingway, and was witnessed with interest by large sections of the crowd.

GRATEFUL THANKS.

After the ceremony tea was provided in the Congregational School for friends from a distance. Coun. Denham, on behalf of the Memorial Committee, expressed thanks to Mr. Whitley and others who had taken part in the ceremony, also to Messrs. Joseph and Charles Smithson. When Mr Horner and he saw Messrs. Smithson, continued the speaker, at the inception of the scheme, and explained the purpose for which the land was required, they let them have the 12 acres at the price offered, and they gave £100 towards the scheme. By their action they had added another link to the chain which bound them with grateful memories to the urban district of Hipperholme. There had been an excellent committee of real workers for the memorial scheme. The expert services of Mr. Longbottom had been appreciated and the monument was a credit to his skill. Mr. Dean, the Council's surveyor, had carried out his work with a zeal which surpassed all praise. The committee owed a real debt to Mr Horner, to whose idea the scheme was really due. Mr. Horner approached him (Mr. Denham) concerning it, and they had worked hand in hand. The whole committee had worked splendidly, as one team. From the financial side also the scheme had been a wonderful success. £3,750 had been subscribed in a district where the population was a little over 4,000. He thought that result would compare favourably with any other place. The Stray would remain an open space forever, so the children in future generations, as well as those of today, would not only get pleasure, but also health through its provision. In according thanks to those who had taken part in that day's proceedings, the Chairman said he could not forget the ex-servicemen, who had attended in such splendid numbers, and he also wished to acknowledge the services which had been rendered by the local special constables in ensuring the success of the arrangements.

Mr. Whitley first of all replied and took the opportunity of congratulating the people of Hipperholme on the form the War Memorial had taken. There was no greater gift a village or town could have than an open space. He wished more of our public spirited citizens would take that view, and when they desired to give anything, he suggested that one of their first thoughts should be: what is the best open space I can give for the children and older people of the future. Mr Whitley added that his chief pleasure that afternoon came from seeing a fine open space belonging to the community forever. A great deal depended on the bringing up of the children, and if they could be impressed with the fact that large pieces of land like that belonged to them, then would come the instinct to protect and not destroy it.

Charles Smithson

Joseph Smithson

(Chris Helme Collection)

Mr. Charles Smithson, representing the late owners of the land, said they felt it a great honour to be asked to take part in that day's impressive public ceremony. One reason why they so readily agreed to the proposal of Mr. Denham and Mr. Horner was because they felt that the object for which the property was to be acquired was one which their uncle, the late Mr. Joshua Smithson (who was the owner of the property for so many years and took a great interest in the welfare of the district), would have approved of, and it would have given him great pleasure to see it carried out. Partly in his memory they so readily agreed to the proposal put before them. It was a fitting thing that the Stray, which had been dedicated for public use and the common good for all time, should be a memorial to the unity of spirit which prevailed throughout the whole community, without class or distinction, during the war. Some 50 years ago, when a boy, he used to play in those fields. At that time the Lightcliffe and Hipperholme district was regarded as a very attractive residential neighbourhood, and it had maintained this reputation as the most attractive district between Bradford and Halifax. He hoped the presentation of the Stray as an open space would help the district to keep that reputation for many generations to come.

Mr. Joseph Smithson associated himself with his brother's expressions of pleasure at being able to do something to make that scheme possible. Though his brother and he had been rather prominently associated with the scheme it should be understood that so far as a considerable portion of the property was concerned it had been acquired with the goodwill of a number of other members of the family who would be glad to be associated in the expression of pleasure that the home of their uncle should have been devoted to a purpose of that kind. It was a happy idea to combine with the unveiling of the memorial the planting of the trees, which, as they grew in life and vigour, would, he hoped unfold a story of peaceful service for the enrichment of the future.

Mr. E. J. Reddie proposed, Mr. C. E. Rose seconded, and Mr. F. M. Horner supported, a resolution of thanks to Coun. Denham for his guidance in bringing the memorial scheme to success. Mr. Horner remarked that Mr. Denham not only possessed tact but also vision and imagination. The whole district owed him a debt of gratitude. They were also indebted to Mr. B. O. Osborn, Mr. Rose and Mr Naylor for the way in which they had met the committee with regard to portions of the land. Coun. Denham, acknowledging the vote, said the memorial would be handed over to the Council for maintenance, but he was going to suggest that a special committee should be appointed to deal with its management, and that some of the workers for the memorial should be co-opted members of that latter committee.

After the ceremony. I cannot identify these gentlemen, but imagine they could include the three custodians of the deeds– Denham, Reddie and Pohlmann – and possibly Francis Horner, the Council's clerk.
(John Illingworth Collection)

Reflection

What inexpressible sadness; what tragedy. Tragedy repeated countless times over much of the world. So many villages, towns and cities changed for ever. Buildings can be replaced. Millions of human beings, young military men in the main, but also civilians of both sexes and all ages, became memories, and are now forgotten, or are names inscribed on cenotaphs, photographs in family albums. How poignant, those messages attached to the floral offerings. 'Never such innocence again.'[59]

The Hipperholme and Lightcliffe Memorial Stray is open, the memorial unveiled.
The crowd disperses.

The photograph on the left shows part of the northern section of Smithson Park sometime between 1915 and 1920. Two points to note, when considering the landscape changes made before the official opening, are that the field slopes gently towards the Leeds and Whitehall Road, and secondly, there is a wall between the park and the road.

The illustration overleaf must have been taken either later on the day of the opening ceremony or on one of the following days. It clearly shows people looking at the flowers in front of the memorial and leaning to read messages on the cards accompanying them. The wall has gone: the vehicle on the left is almost wholly visible, as are the people to the right, ill-defined though they may be. What is well illustrated here is the extent of the banking up of the area around and to each side of the memorial. There are no steps leading to the road, no hedges and no gardens. They were all to follow in the next few years.

(John Illingworth Collection)

A further image (*left*), again showing people reading the dedications on the floral tributes, reinforces these points. The five trees, planted during the ceremony, line the approach to the memorial. On the right, the old oak tree looks the same as it does today, aged, though younger then than now.

(John Illingworth Collection)

Loose Ends

The Hipperholme War Memorial Committee, although containing councillors and being chaired by the chairman of the Council, was a separate body. Details of their minutes are not available, so their progress can only be known insofar as they released details to local newspapers. In particular, we are unaware when the decision, surely important and fundamental, was taken not to include names on the memorial. Was the reason a change of heart or simply a matter of finance? It is a pity that the original intention to inscribe names on the memorial was not followed through.

The first consideration, following the successful opening, was meeting the shortfall. Three months later, on 19th December, Algernon Denham, as chairman of the Council, wrote to Newton Brooke.[60] A further £200 was required to ensure all costs would be met. Denham was 'directed to thank you for your past help, which is much appreciated, and to express the hope that you will give a further and final subscription …' A handwritten note at the foot of the letter says that Denham is donating a further £10 and hopes 'to get 19 others to join me.' No doubt eighteen similar letters were sent out by the Council, signed by the chairman.

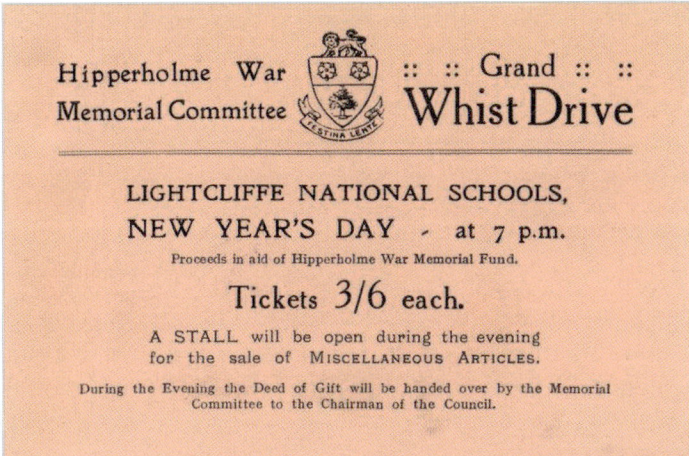

He hopes the money will be raised by 1st January when they are holding a whist drive (he encloses tickets for Brooke) at the end of which they intend to hold 'a little ceremony … for the formal handing over of the deeds.'[61] Smithson Park had been purchased by the war memorial committee. Ownership needed to be transferred from Messrs. Denham, Reddie and Pohlmann to the Hipperholme District Council, which was now responsible for the development and upkeep of the Memorial Stray.

(Chris Helme Collection)

Brooke replies to Denham, enclosing £10 and expressing his confidence that the balance will be raised, although he regrets that he will be 'precluded from the pleasure of attending the Whist Drive on New Year's Day'.

The deeds were successfully transferred, as confirmed by this minute of the War Memorial and Stray Committee of Hipperholme Council, from a meeting of 15 January 1924.

333. Memorial Stray.

Councillor Lumb reported that, on the 1st January, 1924, at a social gathering convened by the Hipperholme War Memorial Stray Committee, he had accepted, on behalf of the Council, the deeds relating to the Stray. On behalf of the Council and the Ratepayers of the District he expressed their thanks to the Officers and Members of the War Memorial Committee and to the Subscribers generally for the magnificent efforts which had been put forward, and which had resulted in the gift to the District of the Smithson's Park, as a Memorial Stray, to be used for the recreation of the public for ever.

Moved by Councillor LUMB,
Seconded by Councillor WOOD,
That the Clerk be instructed to write to the War Memorial Committee thanking them on behalf of the Council, and of the Ratepayers generally for their services.

The final accounts of the war memorial committee, together with the two photographs on p.55, are evidence of the work that had been done to convert pasture land into a public park. The paths, the trees and guards, the seats are clearly in place.

HIPPERHOLME WAR MEMORIAL COMMITTEE.

Statement of Receipts and Expenditure in Provision of War Memorial and Stray

RECEIPTS.	£ s. d.	EXPENDITURE.	£ s. d.
To Subscriptions, including contributions specially earmarked for Seating Accommodation	4,170 18 10	By Purchase of Land	2,681 8 6
„ Bank Interest	26 1 6	„ Erection of Memorial	708 12 0
		„ Manual Labour on Stray	327 0 1
		„ Formation of Footpaths	221 6 1
		„ Legal Charges	66 17 6
		„ Printing and Advertising	46 17 6
		„ Seats	46 16 9
		„ Earthenware Pipes	31 9 5
		„ Team Labour	24 4 9
		„ Trees and Guards	13 14 6
		„ Hire of Band for Opening Ceremony	7 10 0
		„ Bank Charges	3 6 1
			4,179 3 2
		„ Balance, paid over to Ladies' Shelter Committee towards erection of Shelter on Stray	17 17 2
	£4,197 0 4		£4,197 0 4

Audited and found correct.
(Signed) EDGAR SPROAT, AC.A.,
Sproat and Howarth,
Chartered Accountants,
Halifax.
18th June, 1925.
Accounts relating to the above Statement, together with Receipt Books, Invoices and Vouchers, will be open to inspection by any person interested, at the Council Offices, Hipperholme, during the usual office hours.
FRANCIS M. HORNER,
Clerk of the Committee.
NORMAN WOOD,
Chairman, War Memorial and Parks Committee.

(Chris Helme Collection)

I have already commented on the earthenware pipes, which must have been used to install drainage to the area most susceptible to marshy ground and flooding in times of heavy rainfall; in fact, this would be largely the area in the two photographs of the cenotaph above. Much of the labouring costs would have gone to the laying of the pipes.

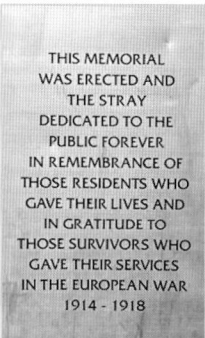

THIS MEMORIAL WAS ERECTED AND THE STRAY DEDICATED TO THE PUBLIC FOREVER IN REMEMBRANCE OF THOSE RESIDENTS WHO GAVE THEIR LIVES AND IN GRATITUDE TO THOSE SURVIVORS WHO GAVE THEIR SERVICES IN THE EUROPEAN WAR 1914 - 1918

It was almost five years since the armistice had been signed, five years during which all the local churches, and a number of other institutions, had unveiled their own memorials. It is difficult to understand why the most powerful organisation in the area should have taken so long, firstly to decide upon a symbol of remembrance, and then to see through the scheme. There is also no record in council minutes, as suggested earlier, of the intriguing decision not to incorporate into the memorial an inscription with the names of those who had died, as this had been an early intention. Was it because the 109 men and one woman had, by late 1923, been commemorated on one or more of the other plaques in the district? The Stray must have been regarded by the councillors of Hipperholme U.D.C. as a sort of unifying emblem. However, the plaque, as can be seen to the left, has wording which does not even identify the area. Again, there is no record of the decision as to the layout of the memorial. The single word 'Hipperholme' could have been divisive; 'Hipperholme, Lightcliffe and Bailiff Bridge' possibly regarded as too lengthy.

CHAPTER 6

THE EARLY YEARS – 1924-39

HIPPERHOLME AND LIGHTCLIFFE, not forgetting Bailiff Bridge, now had a large public park, a 'unique memorial' to those whose lives were lost in the war. Community interest in the Stray was reflected in the thousands who attended the opening ceremony. The vision which led to the cenotaph, and would be further realised by the planting of flower beds and hedges, and more trees, in the coming years, the stone plinth always the focus of this development, has been celebrated by generations of villagers since that September day of a hundred years ago.

Hipperholme Urban District Council became responsible for the development and upkeep of the new open space until, in 1937, it became part of the larger Brighouse authority, and control passed from the council offices on Leeds Road to the town hall in Thornton Square.

At the end of 1923 the Stray had an imposing cenotaph, paths, benches and a few trees. During the early years a shelter and public conveniences were built, the hedges and gardens around the cenotaph were established, playground equipment was provided, and there was further tree planting. In November 1931 the possibility of extending the Stray was even considered, and rejected, when three property owners with land adjoining the park offered to sell at 2s.6d. per square yard.[62]

I propose to follow the progress of each separate aspect of the Stray's upkeep and development through the decisions of the council committee which oversaw almost all aspects of its administration. The War Memorial, Stray and Parks Committee of the Hipperholme Council had been formed in May 1924, and first met in November of that year. In 1931 it became the Parks and Stray Committee. There were always four co-opted members. At the start these were Messrs. Bernard Osborne and Reddie, and Mesdames Bussey and Wakefield. Bussey and Wakefield remained on the committee until the demise of Hipperholme U.D.C. Osborne and Reddie both resigned, to be replaced by Lightcliffe cricketer W. H. 'Bert' Foster and Algernon Denham, who had by then (1931) ceased to be a councillor. Denham was succeeded by David S. Greenwood, another Lightcliffe cricketer, in 1933. With the transfer of control to Brighouse Council, the Stray came under the aegis of its Parks and Cemeteries Committee.

Shelter

In many ways the shelter was, in later years, the focal point of the Stray. All paths led to it, and it stood at the end of an avenue of trees at the head of which was the memorial itself. The credit balance of £17.17s.2d. in the final accounts of the war memorial committee was paid over to the 'Ladies' Shelter Committee'. (At the council meeting in June 1925, Councillor Robinson commented that he was 'sorry that the money was handed back, because the question of lavatory accommodation was getting very serious now, and the money might have helped considerably.') The previous month the Council had decided that 'sanction be given to the Ladies' Shelter Committee to erect a Shelter on the Stray'.[63] It was also recommended 'that the rough work in connection with erection of Shelter, chiefly excavating and rough concreting, be carried out by the Council's employees and that cost price only be charged for the work.' Finally, the council surveyor, Mr. Dean, would be 'allowed to supervise the work … on behalf of the Ladies' Committee.'

At the May council meeting there was debate, and some disagreement, regarding the siting of the shelter. The committee had passed a resolution that 'the proposed shelter be erected on the circular portion of the pathway, in a direct line from the memorial, as recommended by the majority of the Ladies' Committee.' (I take this to indicate the area where three paths met; in fact, where the shelter was eventually erected.) Councillor Robinson explained that 'the idea had been to prevent any obstruction to the view of the Memorial'. 'There would be a perfect view … from the low road [Wakefield Road].' Councillor Hey, however, felt that 'a one-storey building would obstruct the view of the Memorial.' He proposed an amendment that the minute be referred back to the committee for reconsideration. This was seconded and, despite Councillor Bussey's comment that 'a lot of time and thought' had already been given to the matter, and they should abide by the committee's decision (she would also have been a member of the ladies' committee), the amendment was put to the vote. It was defeated.

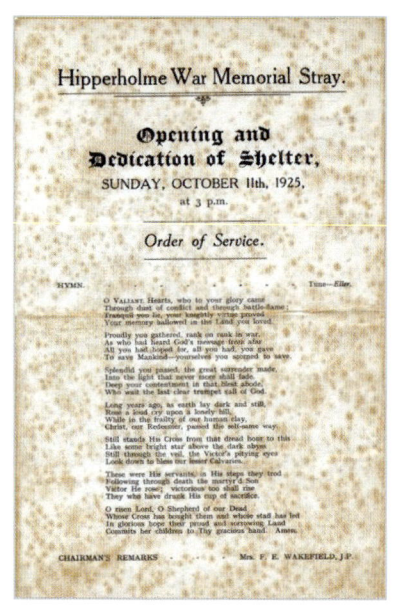

The opening ceremony took place on Sunday, 11 October 1925. Chris Helme has what could be the only surviving programme. It is badly foxed, as can be seen from the opening page *(left)* but the details of the religious service are clear enough:

HYMN 'O Valiant Hearts, who to your glory came …'

CHAIRMAN'S [sic] REMARKS MRS. F. E. WAKEFIELD, J.P.

HYMN 'Fight the good fight …'

OPENING OF SHELTER A. DENHAM, Esq., J.P.

ACCEPTANCE OF SHELTER on behalf of HIPPERHOLME URBAN DISTRICT COUNCIL N WOOD, Esq., J.P.

DEDICATION OF SHELTER [with a repetition of the citation on the memorial] REV. H. L. TAYLOR, M.A.

DEDICATORY PRAYER REV. R. A. SHACKLETON, M.A.

HYMN 'For all the Saints …'

LESSON REV. A. J. FARNSWORTH

HYMN 'O God, our help in ages past …'

THE BLESSING REV. J. H. N. TOMSEN, M.A.

NATIONAL ANTHEM

The programme concluded with an acknowledgement of the organisations who had participated in the opening ceremony:

THE AUGMENTED CHOIRS AND SCHOLARS FROM THE SUNDAY SCHOOLS OF THE DISTRICT WILL ATTEND UNDER THE LEADERSHIP OF L. M. AMBLER, Esq., F.R.C.O.

THE BRIGHOUSE AND RASTRICK TEMPERANCE BRASS BAND WILL ACCOMPANY THE SINGING AND GIVE SELECTIONS AFTER THE SERVICE.

A GENEROUS COLLECTION IS ASKED FOR TO DEFRAY THE EXPENSES OF THE DAY AND TO AID THE SHELTER FUND.

This photograph from the *Brighouse and Elland Echo* shows both Denham and Wakefield addressing the crowd.

(Adapted by Peter Bottomley.)

The same month the Council's Highways, Gas and Public Lighting Committee considered a recommendation of the War Memorial, Stray and Parks Committee that 'the new Shelter … be electrically illuminated … at an approximate cost of £26.' The idea was to connect to the main in Sutherland Road. This was never followed up.

Although not clear from the photograph on the right, taken in the early 1930s, the shelter had seating along the back walls of each of the four compartments. The walls themselves were in glazed deep red brick with a thin lighter band of lime green just below the windows. It was a wonderful building, serving all sorts of purposes, but there were problems of maintenance from the

outset. After only four years, two dozen squares of glass were required to replace broken windows, presumably caused by wilful damage. In 1932 the surveyor submitted samples of safety glass and wire netting for protecting the windows. In November 1929 the committee had asked the Council to provide collapsible gates for closing the shelter at night. By March the following year the surveyor submitted a plan to the Council, who referred the matter back to committee. In June, having reconsidered plans at an estimated cost of £123, it was decided that no further action be taken.

Another early photograph of the shelter.   (Chris Helme Collection)

In February 1932 the surveyor submitted a report on the condition of the shelter. It was decided that he and the chairman would pursue the issues of tiling, painting and 'general renovating'. Tiling was the main concern, and the following month, on the recommendation of the surveyor, the clerk was asked to write to 'Coalbrook Dale Tile Company', the suppliers of the roof-tiles, many of which had 'perished', asking them to 'make good'. In May an independent inspection was carried out by a different company, after which the suppliers were again contacted. The September meeting of the committee heard that Coalbrook had 'without prejudice' agreed to supply 'sufficient hard-burned brindle tiles, free of cost carriage paid to Hipperholme Station'. A month later, the work had been completed, at a cost of £7.10s.0d. In the same month the tenders for painting were considered. That of Mr. B. Hartley, at £3.18s.0d. was accepted.

Public Conveniences

In October 1925 the surveyor was asked to prepare a plan for public conveniences and to suggest a suitable site. Three months later an estimate of £360 was submitted and approved, although no site was recommended. The committee asked the council to include the sum in the estimates for the following financial year, adding that the conveniences were a necessity. Nothing was reported for a year until, in January 1927, the Council was asked by committee to adopt a site 'at the end of Holly Bank Gardens'.

The idea would seem to have been to place the facility near to the gardens and memorial, on the basis that this was the most popular area. If land was to be acquired, it must have been outside the park. There was no building at the time between Holly Bank Gardens (now Holly Bank Drive) and the Congregational church, as can be seen in this extract from the 1922 O.S. map *(adapted by Peter Bottomley)*, so a location at 'the end of Holly Bank Gardens' must have been in the area shaded red. If the site the committee had in mind wasn't available, the recommendation was to build them on the Stray, as close to the proposed site as possible.

In May there was a further obstacle to the planning, and it was resolved that 'owing to the postponement of Main Road Improvements this Committee urge the Council to proceed with the erection of Conveniences on the Stray as a separate scheme without delay.' The surveyor was, at the same time, asked to produce plans and estimates for toilets at the Wakefield Road side of the park. At a full council meeting in early July it was decided that 'Public Conveniences be erected on the Wakefield Road side of the Stray, at an approximate cost of £650, and that application be forthwith made to the Ministry of Health for sanction to borrow that amount.' A sub-committee was set up to 'recommend the site, plans and specification for the same.' The tender of John Coke and Son was accepted before the end of 1927, so the Ministry must have approved the loan.

In what had become the *Brighouse and Elland Echo*, of 23 March 1928, while reviewing the previous twelve months, Councillor Wood said, 'Public conveniences had been erected on the Stray', so they must have been built in the first three months of that year.[64] There is no record of an opening ceremony. The 1932 O.S. map (*left*) shows their exact location, identified as 'Lavs'. The cost must have included the laying of new footpaths. The only further pre-war reference to conveniences concerns the employment of someone to close them at 10.30 p.m. each night. Presumably, although this is not mentioned, the same or another person unlocked them in the mornings.

Public Conveniences, from a postcard dated 1932. The vehicle is parked on Wakefield Road.
(John Illingworth Collection)

Trees and Gardens

The postcard below, again dated 1932, shows the completed gardens around the memorial. I have already commented that when the Stray was opened the land at the Leeds Road border had been banked up. It was bare ground, and in November 1924 it was arranged to seed what was referred to as the 'top level'. However, the following spring this decision was rescinded and, instead of 'sowing down', it was decided to cover the area 'with turf removed from the Sanitary Tip'. Perhaps this was from the council tip at Badger Lane, down the hill from what was then Hipperholme station. As can be seen, the gardens were stacked with bedding plants, shrubs, and privet hedges.

(John Illingworth Collection)

Much of this would have been the work of James Sykes of Oak House, about thirty yards along Leeds Road from the top of the Stray towards Hipperholme crossroads. He submitted a tender of '£16.0s.0d. per annum for the maintenance and planting of flower beds, etc., round the War Memorial.' The tender was accepted by the Council at its meeting of April 1924. In later years, some of these plants would have been germinated along the road: a minute of August 1929 records that 'the offer of the Hipperholme Bowling Club for the use of a piece of land for a cold frame and attention to same at 10s. per annum be accepted.'

The photograph on the right shows Oak House decorated for the coronation of George V, which took place on the date at the bottom of the photo. The house had been built for James and Lily Ann Sykes in the mid-1890s.

(Jayne Caswell Collection)

At the beginning of 1927 the bank alongside Sutherland Road was dug up, weeded, and additional shrubs planted. The February meeting heard that Charles Kershaw had offered to plant eighty shrubs at one shilling each. This must have been the border of laurel and holly that still flourishes there *(left, in May 2023).*

The following year it was decided that steps above the memorial, leading to the road, be erected. (These are visible, although not clearly, in the photograph on the next page.) The layout of the upper area has not changed since that time, although in September 1931 a sub-committee was appointed to 'consider and report' on the 'gardens adjoining Whitehall Road'. Planting, replanting, and replacing trees was an almost annual occupation during these early years.

New steps to Leeds & Whitehall Road, behind the memorial. The path in the foreground, worn by footfall, no longer exists. (John Illingworth Collection)

The November 1924 meeting of the War Memorial, Stray and Parks Committee was its first. Previously, matters seem usually to have been dealt with at the Sanitary and Water Committee. At this inaugural meeting one senses a resolve to make the Stray, within the Council's modest means, as attractive as possible. It was decided to place a dozen 'suitably inscribed pots' for the use of people bringing flowers, although there's no suggestion as to whether these would be close to the memorial or at different places in the park. The committee also resolved to purchase five extra trees to complete the avenue from the memorial to the 'centre of the Stray'. (Most of these limes are still flourishing.)

Reports of damage to installations or vegetation on the Stray is disappointing to read, but it has to be borne in mind that this is exactly the sort of thing that is reported to committee. There is never mention of how many people enjoyed their new facility and relished time spent there. However, a letter the following summer from George Walsh 'regarding damage to trees etc.' strikes a sour note as there were few trees and the park was less than two years old. Apparently, the damage was caused to one of the Smithson Park oak trees. The Council asked the public to help them 'preserve the amenities and to stop boys and girls, or whoever was doing damage to the trees and shrubbery … He would appeal to the boys to give the old trees the consideration they would give to old people.' Walsh is assured that the matter will receive the committee's attention. The following April iron guards were placed around the trees on the avenue. Joseph Walsh, prominent local architect, and enthusiastic promoter of the Dog Bridge walk / Hipperholme recreation ground memorial idea, had a brother George, who was seventy-six in 1925. Joseph also had a son George, twenty-six at the time. Both were likely correspondents.[65]

In January 1926 twelve trees were removed from King George V Park and replanted alongside the Wakefield Road border of the Stray. A year later the surveyor was asked to remove them as they were in an 'unsatisfactory condition'; if any were likely to survive, he should plant them elsewhere. At the same time, an offer from Charles Kershaw to donate six acacias and six Wheatley elms was accepted. But nine months later the surveyor reported that 'several of the newly planted trees alongside Wakefield Road had failed owing to excessive water in the land.' The trees would be replaced but he recommended that the area be drained before this was done. It was decided to ask the council for permission to exceed the year's estimate for drainage provision. At the same time bronze name plates were affixed to the five trees planted at the opening ceremony.

The Wakefield Road border of the Stray. There has been no attempt to plant trees so I assume this to have been taken in 1924 or 1925. The car probably belonged to Dr. John Gatherer Brown of Knowl House, grandfather of Rose Pickles. (Is it the same car that's parked on Knowle Top Road – see p. 25.)Note the new Lydgate House wall, background left. When the 1923 sale was made, its gardens were extended to include some of the Smithson Park land.

(Rose Pickles Collection)

In 1930 the Council's accountant applied for a grant to help with tree planting, but received the discouraging response from the Forestry Commission that grants were only available where five acres were to be planted in one season, with 1,400 to 2,100 trees per acre. The committee took the matter no further. Trees continued to be planted, sometimes as replacements for ones that had died. The same year it was decided that an 'experienced gardener' should be responsible for replacing dead trees, but that 'Councillors Holgate and Lawson, in consultation with the Surveyor, arrange the type of tree and place of planting.'

The experienced gardener must have done his job well because there are no further reports of arboreal ailment; in fact, no reference to trees until late in 1935, when the chairman of the Council, Tom Holgate, was asked to plant two oak trees *(left, in May 2023)*. One was to celebrate his own thirty years of continuous service on the Council, in recognition of which he was presented with a miniature silver spade by Algernon Denham. The other was to commemorate 'the twenty-fifth Anniversary of the Accession to the Throne of their Majesties, King George V and Queen Mary.'

Councillor Holgate thanked members.

A fortnight later an offer was received from Charles Dickinson to 'defray the cost of a line of trees on either side of one of the pathways to further commemorate the anniversary of Their Majesty's [sic] reign.' The offer was accepted. Mr. Dickinson specified that he would like the trees to be planted 'on either side of the pathway nearest to Wakefield Road leading to Sutherland Road.'

This vague description is clarified by an albeit poor reproduction of a photograph which appeared in the *Brighouse and Elland Echo* of 20 March 1936. (Shelter in the background.) We are told that 'Mr. C. E. Dickinson formally planted the last of an avenue of twenty-five copper beeches which he has presented to the district.' I think Mr. Dickinson's assistant is Algernon Denham. This identifies the pathway as being the only one which ran parallel to Wakefield Road. Ten years later, on 17 June 1946 the Brighouse Council's Parks Committee resolved that 'the Town Clerk be instructed to ask Mr. C. E. Dickinson of "Stoneyhurst" if he would consent to the copper beech trees presented by him and planted on the Stray being replaced as they had made little progress since they were planted.'

Cherry trees, beautifully blossoming every late April and early May, have aligned this pathway for decades. Many have been replaced but there are still eight or nine of the originals, a number of which are in the photograph to the right, taken in May 2023, looking across from Sutherland Road to the wall at the edge of what was Lydgate House, is now Lydgate Park.

(Author's Collection)

Twelve months after the planting ceremony the committee heard that Dickinson (*left*) 'was desirous of giving further trees to extend the Avenue of Trees on the Stray', to commemorate the coronation of George VI. (The coronation preparations had, of course, originally been intended for the crowning of Edward VIII.) The surveyor had estimated the number required at twenty-one. A sub-committee was appointed 'to interview Mr. Dickinson to ascertain his wishes in the matter and thereafter the details of the ceremony be left with the Coronation Committee.' The *Halifax Courier* of 19th April gives a full account of the ceremony.

'Ten of the trees were planted officially by Mr. J. W. Turner, former Chairman of the Council; Mrs. Bussey; Mrs. Wakefield, J.P.; Mr. W. H. Foster and Mr. D. Greenwood, co-opted members of the Parks and Stray

Committee; and the following schoolboys: Milton Aspinall (Ebenezer Methodist Sunday School, Bailiff Bridge), Ernest Barrett (Lightcliffe Congregational Sunday School), Jeffrey Dawe (Hipperholme Methodist Sunday School), Donald Sykes (Lightcliffe Church Sunday School), and John R. Walker (Hipperholme Grammar School).'

A schoolboy plants a tree. (Brighouse Echo.)

Councillor Roe proposed a vote of thanks to Mr. Dickinson, at the same time appealing to children to 'take care of the trees and to see they were not damaged.' This was seconded by J. W. Houseman, head of Hipperholme Grammar School. He remarked that Mr. Dickinson was an old boy of the school; he also 'appealed to the boys and girls to protect the trees.' The trees were blessed by the Rev. J. S. Mclaughlan. Mr. Dickinson responded that 'his idea of inviting the boys to plant trees was to give them an added interest in the Stray.' He also suggested the formation of a local watch committee to 'report irregularities' in the park.

In the autumn of 1931, a sub-committee had been convened to consider three offers to sell land to the Council, so that the Stray could be extended in its north-west corner. Councillor Denham reported to the November meeting of the Parks and Stray Committee that he had received 'tentative offers' of 2s.6d. per square yard, as follows:

> 1820 square yards from 'Bancroft's representatives';
> 1251 square yards from Mr. Sykes;
> 2647 square yards from Mrs. Hind.

The plan on the right forms part of a 1908 transaction involving a portion of Smithson Park.[66] (Not the whole of the area in pink; just the scruffily pencilled-off square next to Wakefield Road, on which the houses Netherfield and Rylstone would soon be built.) In 1931 Louis John Bancroft lived at Craigmore, Holly Bank Drive, and Lillian Annie Hind at Elm Grange, a large detached house alongside Leeds and Whitehall Road, off the map to the left. Oak House was built by James Sykes in 1895, and he and his wife were still in residence in 1931. Whoever drew the plan in 1908 was incorrect as regards ownership of land and has failed to record the presence of Oak

House. In correspondence some years ago with James Sykes's great granddaughter, Jayne Caswell, I learned that Mr. Sykes, her great grandfather, had a market garden on the land between the house and the Stray. It's easy to see how acquisition of these two parcels of land (Bancroft and Sykes) would extend the Stray, but not clear where Mrs. Hind fits into the proposal, unless the Hinds had, in the previous twenty-three years, acquired the field (for such it was at that time) in the 1908 ownership of Emma Whiteley. This is possible as the field was adjacent to Elm Grange.

Two resolutions were put forward to the meeting: that Mrs. Hind be offered 2s.6d. per square yard for her land; Messrs. Sykes and Bancroft 2s. for theirs. Neither resolution was carried.

Playground Equipment

In the estimates submitted to council by the War Memorial, Stray and Parks Committee in February 1927 was an item of £80 for playground appliances. The Council was recommended to:

'(a) set apart the western portion of the Stray for the purpose of a playground for young people on weekdays …

(b) as a first instalment of equipment, there be provided football goalposts, two sets of swings, each having six seats, and the "Ocean Wave", as supplied by Messrs. C. Wicksteed of Kettering, at an approximate cost of £80.'

In the event, £50 was allocated. The members of the committee visited Shibden Park to inspect their appliances, as a result of which, in September, they ordered 'One set of six swings, small size, and one plank swing, small size, together with one set of goal posts for football.' These were to be placed 'on the Western portion of the Stray.'

The plank swing, presumably a generic name for the 'Ocean Wave', still there in the 1950s and 60s, was known to local children as a 'rant'. It was a lethal piece of equipment that could be swung backwards and forwards until it almost touched the supports at the top of the structure.

The photograph on the right shows a contraption identical to the 'rant' on the Stray.

In 1930 the committee wished to complete the equipment 'by the purchase from Charles Wicksteed & Co., Ltd., of a forty-foot slide, a bay of three swings with cradles and locks for same at an estimated cost of £60.0s.0d.' It was also decided to pursue the possibility of a grant from the Carnegie United Kingdom Trust to assist with the outlay. The application was successful and the council received the maximum of one-third of the cost, which amounted to £20. The photograph on the previous page shows the equipment at a much later date, not long before demolition. The slide and two sets of swings are, however, the structures that were set in place almost a hundred years ago, though the 'baby' swings have newer, plastic, cradles and the framework is multi-coloured rather than that deep, ubiquitous mid-twentieth-century green.

Seating, Paths and Lighting

In April 1926, when the seats had been in place no longer than thirty months, the surveyor was asked to arrange for their painting and renovation 'as necessary'. At the same meeting the committee was informed that metal guards had been obtained for all trees forming the avenue from the shelter to the memorial. A year later the Highways Committee was asked 'to purchase two Seats and place same on the Stray adjoining Wakefield Road.' In July 1929 '4 "Ornate" heavy Park Seats, 10 feet wide' were purchased from Wicksteeds. These were to replace four of those on the main avenue. The four seats closest to the camera in the photograph below are different in style from those nearer the shelter and could well be the four in question. The following year all seats were to be renovated, cleaned and painted again, by the Council's own workmen. There is no further reference to the tree guards until 1936, when they were to be 'scraped and painted'.

Benches and tree guards in the early 1930s.   *(John Illingworth Collection)*

The paths around the Stray were well constructed, befitting an outlay of £221.6s.1d., the equivalent of £17,000 after a century of inflation. However, in 1927 the surveyor was authorised 'to raise and repair sunken paths in the vicinity of the Memorial.' This would have been a reflection, not on initial workmanship, but on the fact that the paths were built on the area towards the road which had been raised above the natural level of Smithson Park. Their overall quality is borne out by the fact that there is no further reference to them in the minutes of the Hipperholme council up to its dissolution in 1937.

The early winters would have been dark ones on the Stray. In November 1924 the Public Lighting Committee was asked 'to erect at least four lamps in suitable positions.' The next reference to lighting is in a minute of early 1926, when the same committee accepted the quote from Electrical Distribution of Yorkshire, Ltd. of 10s. plus 1½d. for 'current supplied for lamps on the Stray.' This must have been requested as part of the costing of the project, since the eventual lamps were gas, not electric. In November 1931 there was provision for three lamps to be placed, at a cost of £16.6s.8d., 'in the positions discussed'. Decisions didn't necessarily lead to prompt action. The following October it was resolved that 'the additional lamps be proceeded with and that the Halifax Corporation Gas Works Committee be written to asking if they would be prepared to lay the main for the additional lamps.' If these three lamps were 'additional', there must already have been some in place.

Before   *After*

I think that the original intention to install four lamps was carried out, but somewhat later than hoped, possibly through affordability. Two were placed at each end of the 'avenue' between the shelter and the memorial (see illustration on previous page), and two above the memorial, as above. Both these illustrations show similarly well-established vegetation. *'Before'* has no lamps, so they were not installed in the first few years after the opening, as the gardens between the memorial and the road were being planted and nurtured at that time, but they must have been in place by November 1931, otherwise the reference to 'additional' lamps is meaningless.

Two of the additional three are visible in the illustration to the left. They are south of the shelter. One of the originals can also be seen, next to the shelter at the bottom of the 'avenue'. I think the original four must have been installed only shortly before the decision for additional lighting.

(John Illingworth Collection)

I contacted Philip Tordoff, a man who knows about such things.[67] He suggested the style of the lamps was 'vintage Halifax', and referred me to Dorron Harper, an expert.[68] I wrote to Dorron, enclosing the *'After'* photograph above. He replied promptly, agreeing that the lamps were vintage Halifax, adding 'the style of the lantern, which incorporates a panel of opaque white (known as "opal") glass in the head, suggests the late Victorian period', as does the pattern of the 'bi-colour cast iron column.' However, the Newbridge automatic clockwork controller, 'dates the picture to the early thirties … but the late twenties is not out of the question.' Dorron suggests that the lamps were 'imported from some other part of the town, perhaps as the result of an upgrade somewhere else.' He adds that the Newbridge controller was fitted with a burner and two mantles, which suggests to him that 'the Stray pathway was obviously considered important as a route at night.' The livery would be 'a variation of green and cream or a stone colour, with a green lantern.' (In my recollection, because the lamps were still there in the 1950s, green was a predominant colour. And they were certainly still gas, as it was possible to temporarily extinguish them with a well-aimed snowball.)

Mowing

Trees die, paint flakes and fades. Some of time's inevitabilities can be overlooked by a beleaguered management, but grass keeps on growing and, in a public park, needs to be kept in check. Records of the upkeep of the Stray really only begin with the first meeting of the War Memorial, Stray and Parks Committee in November 1924. At that meeting the surveyor, Mr. Dean, was asked to 'prepare a specification in respect of work necessary for the future upkeep of the Memorial Stray.' This suggests that matters had been allowed to take a natural course during 1924. He was also asked to 'obtain tenders for a suitable one-horse mowing machine.'

The surveyor reported back to the committee three months later. There had evidently been decisions taken off-record as the minutes make clear. Firstly, he 'submitted Tenders for Mowing Machines of various kinds.' It was decided that 'a Green's Perfection Mower be purchased … for £58.10s.0d.' However, this purchase was only to be carried out 'failing arrangements with the Lightcliffe Golf Club for Mowing the Stray with their Ransome Mower.' Mr. Dean also submitted tenders for the upkeep of the Stray, 'as per duties scheduled by the Surveyor' and it was resolved to accept that of Mr. B. Wilkinson in the sum of £45.10s.0d.

1925 was evidently a summer of discontent as regards keeping the grass cropped. In June the surveyor reported 'certain difficulties in obtaining Machine belonging to Lightcliffe Golf Club.' He was authorised to 'hire a one-horse Mowing Machine and commence work as soon as possible.' This must have been done because at the Council meeting that month Councillor Hey asked 'why the hay from the Stray could not have been sold.'[69] He was told that the hay had not been of any great value and 'the committee felt that if they could get the hay taken away and the Stray cleaned and raked, they were not doing so badly.' In July there is a puzzling committee decision that 'the Surveyor endeavour to hire the Lightcliffe Golf Club Mower and carry out the work … when convenient.' The next reference is in October, when Mr. Dean is to 'arrange to mow the Stray at an early date, and hire a one-horse mower for the purpose.'

An intriguing light is cast on the dialogue with the Lightcliffe golf club in Grayham Mitchell's history.[70] Under the chapter heading 'Jottings from Green Meetings', there is an entry for 10 February 1925, when it was agreed that the club should loan their Triplex mower to the Parks Department of the Halifax Urban District Council for a charge of 15 shillings per day. Halifax U.D.C. would have to provide their own man and horse to work the machine. Did the negotiations between the Hipperholme surveyor and golf club founder simply through money? Or was there friction between the management personnel of golf club and council?

In January 1926 the committee became decisive. A one-horse 'Albion' mower was to be purchased at an approximate cost of £22. This amount was to be included in their estimates for 1926-7. Also, a roller was to be hired (presumably not from the golf club) and the Stray 'thoroughly' rolled. At the same meeting Mr. Wilkinson was again employed, on the same terms.

What happened during the summer of 1926 is a mystery as, inexplicably, nothing further was recorded until May 1927, when Mr. Dean reported the successful trial of a Ransome Triple Mower. The committee recommended its purchase 'provided the Council will increase the amount of estimate allotted to the committee by £50.' This was referred back at a full council meeting, and it was September before further consideration was given to the matter, when it was left over until the preparation of estimates for 1928-9.

Although there is no reference in committee minutes, a purchase must have been made in the spring of 1928, as the governors of Hipperholme Grammar School enquired about the loan of 'the Council's Triple Mowing Machine for the purpose of mowing the Grammar School field.' This was agreed on three conditions:

(1) The Council's workmen have charge of the machine.
(2) The Grammar School be responsible for any damage to the machine.
(3) A charge of 5/- per hour be made with a minimum of £1.

Five shillings an hour seems excessive when compared with the golf club's fifteen shillings for the day, but the Council was providing the grammar school with both machine and men. This is Hipperholme Council's final reference to mowing, and there are none in the Brighouse minutes up to the outbreak of war in 1939.

The committee decided, for 1928, that instead of entering into a contract for gardening work, they would appoint a 'whole time Gardener for the War Memorial and Stray and King George V Park, at a wage of £2.15s.0d. per week.' This would amount to £143 for the year, a significant increase in outlay on the previous year when the combined amounts for the contracts for the two parks was £90.10s.0d. The man appointed, as would be revealed by later events, was William Iredale.

An early gardener employee on the Stray was Jim Hudson, remembered with affection by John Millington as a friend of his family.[71] A gardener before the war, Jim carried the legacy of his service in France with injuries that lasted a lifetime. He and his wife lived on Syke Lane, 'second house on the left going down'. There was no hut on the Stray for storage of tools and equipment until the 1950s, so Jim carried his tackle wrapped in sacking on the crossbar of his bicycle. (John Millington says that the hut in the north-west corner of the Stray appeared during his two years of national service, 1954-5.) The details of the early gardeners' duties were not specified. There is a cryptic minute from November 1929, when 'a suggestion for alteration of the Gardener's hours to enable him to spend more time actually on the Gardens' was considered. Presumably, hours were used up in the repair of damage to the shelter and seating, and perhaps in painting. Whatever the issue, it was decided that no alteration be made.

Law and Order

In July 1925 draft by-laws for the Stray had been approved by the Council. After the required notice was posted in local newspapers, they were submitted to the Minister of Health. Three months later the surveyor reported that they had been approved by the ministry, and copies were printed. (See Appendix 2.) One practice they certainly covered was the riding of bicycles. It was forbidden. Indeed, there had been a complaint at the June council meeting that year of the 'riding of bicycles on the Stray's footpaths'.[72]

In June 1929 the full council received a report from the West Riding Police 'regarding boys riding bicycles on the footpaths at the Stray.' The *Echo* reported that 'two Hove Edge youths, aged …16 and 17, had been seen riding down the Stray on June 10. The lads cycled towards the shelter and round it, although children were playing there. On seeing the police, however, they dismounted. The youths were warned. Several complaints had been made to the police regarding the practice. Coun. N. Wood commented that they were not just little lads that committed the offence. Youths cycled down the paths and developed a big speed, which was dangerous to others. He knew the slope was tempting, but the practice would have to be stopped.' The police were to be 'thanked for their vigilance in the matter'. Furthermore, 'the parents of the boys concerned be written to demanding an apology and a promise that the offence would not be again committed.' On receipt of such an apology no further action would be taken. The following month the clerk reported that apologies had been received, and that he would pass these on to the police.

This was the prelude to a couple of years of conflict between the Council and unnamed transgressors. In June 1930 'Complaints were made by Members of the Committee regarding the playing of Golf upon the Stray.' This was evidently a matter of some seriousness, as the decision was made that the 'games of golf, Tip-cat and Knur and Spell be prohibited as causing discomfort to persons on the Stray and as likely to cause undue interference with the reasonable and proper use of the Stray by other persons.' As a measure of the committee's resolve to cut out the playing of games in a large public park 'The Accountant was further instructed to arrange Notice Boards prohibiting the above games in all Parks and Recreation Grounds under the control of the Council.'

At the same June meeting the committee heard that complaints had been made regarding 'certain conduct in the Stray and the advisability of controlling persons using the Stray.' The conduct is not specified, but it is hardly likely to be golf, tipcat or knur and spell. Nevertheless, persons had to be controlled, and the Council was recommended to appoint a 'Park Ranger for all Parks and Playgrounds for an estimated working week of 40 hours.' Whatever the nature of the offensive conduct, it was clearly rife in the neighbourhood's public open spaces. The Council referred the matter back to the committee, who decided the following month that 'one of the Council's regular workmen be offered the sum of 5s. per week for patrolling the Stray between the hours of 7 p.m. and 11 p.m. for a period of three months.' So, the 'conduct' was taking place in the evenings, and it was not anticipated it would continue into the winter months. In early September the surveyor informed the committee that he had 'appointed Mr. William Iredale, the Council's Gardener, as part-time Ranger.' At the end of that month the surveyor 'read a report [from the Ranger] regarding conduct on the Stray. It was requested that 'further reports contain the names and addresses of any offenders.'

Three months later, at its December meeting, the committee received another report, via the surveyor. Details are not revealed, but they did not please the members, who 'express[ed] dissatisfaction with the services of the Gardener and Park Ranger and recommend[ed] to the Council at the Annual Revision of Salaries that a change be made.' At the same meeting it was resolved that 'owing to reports of unseemly behaviour on the Stray that police action be sought and that any prosecution arising … be supported by the Council.' 'Unseemly behaviour' between the hours of 7 and 11 p.m. on summer nights. One can only speculate. And perhaps sympathise with those paid five shillings a week to eradicate such behaviour. Councillor Gelder voted against both resolutions.

'Conduct on the Stray' continued to preoccupy the committee into 1931. In January 'The Accountant was instructed to extract from the Council's Stray Byelaws such Byelaws as may be considered necessary for publication on the Stray after first consulting the Police Authority.' The 'hours and working conditions of the Gardener and Park Ranger', who must have been retained, were also considered, and the surveyor was requested to reorganise them. This was quickly followed up and, in February, having submitted his suggested working arrangements, the surveyor was asked to 'arrange for some person or persons to open and close the King George V Park and close the Stray Conveniences at a sum not exceeding Five Shillings per week for the two duties.' One assumes the Stray 'Lavs' would be opened in the mornings by the gardener. The accountant reported on his meeting with the police, as a result of which 'a copy of the Stray Byelaws be mounted and published on the Stray in a suitable case and position.'

Three months was all it took before offenders were apprehended, when, following a report from the West Riding Police of two breaches of the by-laws 'affecting the play centre at the Stray', a letter of apology was read and accepted. There is no reference to anything untoward occurring during the months of that summer. However, the problem had not disappeared and, in November, the committee chairman reported that Mr. Harry Dring had been appointed Park Ranger for the Stray at 7s.6d. per week, a 50% increase on the remuneration of his predecessor. His duties were to include 'looking after the conveniences and equipment and patrolling the Stray when necessary.' After three months his wage was increased to ten shillings.

There were to be further cycling offenders, and an expression of regret was no longer regarded as sufficient penance. The *Halifax Courier* of 6 June 1931 reported that 'Herbert Dyson, a motor driver, of Wyke, and Gilbert Leach, a creeler, of Wyke, who pleaded guilty to riding bicycles on the Stray … were fined 5s. each at the West Riding Halifax Court today.'

Matthew Fitton rides his bike on the Stray in 1982. Fifty years earlier this would have cost him five shillings and a police record.

(David and Sheila Fitton Collection)

Francis Horner, appearing on behalf of the Council, told the court that 'the shelter on the Stray had been subject to acts of vandalism and rowdyism.' He did not wish to make the present defendants scapegoats, but pointed out that, whereas in the past an apology had been accepted, the police had been instructed to prosecute in future.

There is only one further reference to contraventions of the by-laws during the 1930s, and this is an activity of a different nature. In July 1933 the clerk was asked to write to Mrs. Greenway of Ivy Terrace, St. Giles Road, (Alice Greenway is at 2, Ivy Terrace in the 1931 Electoral Register) to the effect that it was 'contrary to the Byelaws relating to the Stray for a stall to be erected thereon without permission of the Council.' G. L. Greenway, 'Pastry Cook and Confectioner', had two shops at the time, one on Denholmegate Road, Hipperholme, the other at the end of Ivy Terrace. She supplied 'Fresh Baked Breads and Confectionery for Every Occasion. For afternoon tea, luncheon, breakfast, supper parties, you can have every kind of bread and sweetmeat baked for your own particular occasions, made of the same ingredients and in the same way as you would bake them yourself. Place a standing order today and have your orders brought to the door.'[73] We must assume that, apart from failing to prevent the minor transgression of Mrs. Greenway, Mr. Dring effectively carried out his duties.

After responsibility for the upkeep of the Stray passed to the new Brighouse Council in 1937, there is one reference, in June 1938, to activities, and the offenders here would seem to be a council employee or employees. Mr. H. L. Mollett of Lightcliffe wrote to say that 'his son together with other small boys had been stopped from playing cricket on the upper end of the Stray.' He asked for the Parks and Allotment Committee's ruling. He was informed that 'no objection be raised to the playing of cricket … provided it is not played near any footpath or to the danger or discomfort of other users of the Stray.'

Cricket on the Stray in the mid-1930s.

It is easy to be flippant about the apparent over-reaction to the playing of ball games, but we must remember that the Stray was created as a memorial. Families and friends of those who died were very much a part of the community and awareness of the significance of this open space would never leave them.

Band Concerts

'The brass band represents one of the most remarkable working-class cultural achievements in European history', writes Dave Russell.[74] He quotes estimates of the number of bands in the late nineteenth century as being anything between 30,000 and 40,000. Although the movement was nationwide, the greatest concentration, and the highest quality, was undoubtedly in the coalfields and textile areas of the northern counties. Yorkshire and Lancashire bands dominated the major championships at Belle Vue and Crystal Palace. The tradition of the park concert was established by the 1850s as part of 'a method of bringing wholesome entertainment to the poorest members of society.'[75] This aim was perhaps only partially successful, and Russell suggests that the Sunday afternoon brass band concert was as likely to attract those with a 'desire to display their clothes' as the originally intended audience.[76]

If the late Victorian and Edwardian eras were the heyday of the brass band movement, it still flourished during and after the First World War. Indeed, it remains a significant musical genre to this day, even if changing industrial practices have been largely responsible for a decrease in the number of bands. The opening of the Stray provided opportunities for local bands, and these were taken up by, predominantly, the Brighouse and Rastrick Temperance Band (yet to discard 'Temperance' in favour of plain 'Brass') and the Clifton and Lightcliffe Brass Band. The latter changed titles several times in the first decade of performing on the Stray. In 1926 they were Clifton Brass Band, in 1928 Clifton Prize band, in 1930 Clifton and Lightcliffe Prize Band, until, in 1932, they had become Clifton and Lightcliffe Brass Band, which they remain. The addition of Lightcliffe to their name came about through the intervention of

Newton Brooke. In the late 1920s the band was in danger of folding through lack of money. Mr. Brooke offered to provide new uniforms and a band rehearsal room on condition they added Lightcliffe to their name. This would have been an easy decision. Clifton and Lightcliffe Brass Band still rehearse in their Bailiff Bridge band room.

Clifton and Lightcliffe Prize Band, resplendent in new uniforms, photographed in the grounds of Crow Nest in the early 1930s. Newton Brooke is on the front row, to the right of the bandsman who is presumably the first cornet. To the left of the cornet player is Sam Briggs. The photographer would have had his back to the mansion.

(Chris Helme Collection)

On 10 July 1925 the *Echo* reported that 'Under the conductorship of Mr. F. Berry, Brighouse and Rastrick Temperance Band gave two high-class programmes before large assemblies at the Stray, Lightcliffe, on Sunday afternoon and evening. The proceeds were in aid of the band funds.' Lee Mount Band and Southowram Prize Band also gave concerts. It is most likely that the performances, on Sunday afternoons or evenings, took place in front of the memorial in the horseshoe-shaped area bordered by stone benches, although the proximity of the shelter is another possible location. Bands made a collection and 10% of the receipts above £4 were taken by the Council. In 1926 the Brighouse and Rastrick gave two concerts on Whit Sunday, in the afternoon and evening. The Council asked them to give 50% of their takings to the Cancer Research Fund Campaign. They took £18.2s.1d. After the 10% deduction had been applied, £7.15s.2d. was donated. However, in May 1928, the committee decided that concerts could be held without charge.[77] In 1932 they must have felt that the Stray was underused for entertainment as they decided to contact musical organisations in the district to enquire if any of them wished to give performances.

BRIGHOUSE & RASTRICK BAND. BELLE VUE CHAMPIONS 1929. 1932-3-4
WINNERS OF TROPHIES & CASH PRIZES VALUE OVER £10,000 FROM 1928 TO 1934

The Brighouse and Rastrick Band had dropped the 'Temperance' from their title in 1928. Could there have been a connection here with the success of the following years? (*Chris Helme Collection*)

Other Ceremonies

The wide open spaces and well-kept gardens of the Stray, together with the dignified monument, made it an ideal venue for outdoor gatherings. In October 1935 General R. E. Sugden presented a standard to the Hipperholme, Lightcliffe and Northowram branch of the British Legion. In relating that representatives of the legion had recently visited Germany, he added that 'If we all try to spread this spirit of comradeship all over Europe, we shall do more towards getting peace than anything else.' Rev. R. Machon of Halifax performed the dedication ceremony.

A parade and service, hosted by the Brighouse and Elland Division of the Girl Guides Association, took place on 14 May 1939. The plans were for the parade to assemble at 'Whitehall corner' and, accompanied by the Clifton and Lightcliffe Brass Band, march along Leeds and Whitehall Road to the Stray where they would 'take up their appointed positions'. The service, commencing at 3.30 p.m., was to be conducted by the Rev. Canon Taylor and the Rev. E. H. Hardy, to be followed by an address by Rev. G. H. Marshall, vicar of Ossett, former vicar of St. Augustine's, Halifax. The ceremony was to conclude with a march past the county commissioner, the Hon. Lady Ingleby. Guides and scouts from other divisions were to be 'cordially invited', and a collection taken in aid of nursing associations in the division. An ominous note was added: 'If wet, the service will be held in Lightcliffe Church.'

The *Courier* report of the event was headlined 'Cloudburst During Open-air Service', and continued that the ceremony 'had to be abandoned towards the end owing to what was almost a cloudburst, and during the singing of the last hymn those present had to scamper for shelter.' There were 'about 400 Guides and 100 Scouts', as well as the band, with instruments, many officials, and presumably families of the children, and spectators. The four compartments of the small shelter would have been crowded and cosy until the downpour ended.

CHAPTER 7

WORLD WAR TWO

Trenches on the Stray

IN SEPTEMBER 1938 there was a real German threat to peace in Europe when, on the 17th of the month, Hitler attacked Sudetenland, part of Czechoslovakia forming a mountainous border region between that country and Germany. The anxiety which this caused in Britain can be illustrated by the digging of trenches in local parks, including the Stray. The main fears of the time were gas attacks and air raids, although it is difficult to understand how a trench on the Stray could prevent either, or cope with their effects. It has been suggested to me that, in the event of an air attack, the trenches could be used for sheltering from shrapnel.

From the Brighouse & Elland Echo of 7 October 1938. The caption read: 'SEPTEMBER – During the crisis A.R.P. [Air Raid Precautions] work came into prominence and trenches were dug on the Stray, Lightcliffe, and in other parts of the borough.'

(The trench was at the N.E. corner of the Stray, looking down towards the 'avenue'.)

At the end of the month an agreement was signed at Munich between Germany, France, Britain and Italy that Sudetenland should be ceded to Germany, in order to appease them, on the understanding that this was the limit of Hitler's ambitions. The British prime minister, Neville Chamberlain, returned to London in triumph, brandishing a paper signed by him and Hitler. The British people, or at least those of the Calder valley, were satisfied that the threat of war had been lifted, and four months later, in January 1939, wished to fill in the trenches. Following a meeting of the Calder Valley Joint Air Raid Precautions Committee, the Brighouse borough engineer 'was instructed to apply to the County Surveyor for consent to fill in the trench on the Stray, which was dug during the recent crisis.' Consent was duly granted, and communicated to the air raid precautions committee in March.

Outbreak of War

On 1 September 1939 Hitler invaded Poland. On the morning of Sunday, 3 September, the British ambassador in Berlin handed the German government a note demanding an undertaking, to be received by 11 a.m., that Germany would withdraw its troops from Poland. As Chamberlain said, in his Home Service address to the nation, "… no such undertaking has been received … consequently this country is at war with Germany." The war to end wars had done no such thing.[78] For six years everyday life would be transformed.

The Stray was an obvious location for the 'Dig for Victory' campaign, set up by the Ministry of Agriculture. As well as people turning over their own gardens to vegetables, open spaces everywhere were transformed into allotments. In January 1941 a representative of the War Agriculture Committee had 'urged the cultivation' of four portions of land, including the Stray, following an interview with Brighouse's parks superintendent. However, the Parks Committee resolved that 'no action be taken with regard to the ploughing up of the Stray.' Nor was there any suggestion of re-digging the trenches of 1938.

In April 1942 the medical officer in charge of the first aid post at Hipperholme requested permission to use a portion of the Stray for practices for the mobile gas decontamination unit, which was located in premises behind Hipperholme library. This was granted. The threat of a gas attack was taken so seriously by the government that they decided every man, woman and child should have their own respirator, or gas mask. Scientists at Porton Down designed the model that was eventually issued, and in 1936 a disused mill in Blackburn became an assembly plant. By the time of the Munich Crisis of September 1938 more than thirty million masks had been manufactured. Shortly after the outbreak of war thirty-eight million were distributed throughout the entire population.

By 1939 Brighouse Council had administered the Stray for two years. It is clear from council minutes that it received less formal attention than had been the case when it was run by the Hipperholme U.D.C., although it could reasonably be argued that its teething problems were over. It had its shelter, its toilets, its gardens were well developed, the paths lined with trees. It was self-sufficient as regards maintenance. The changes brought about on the Stray by war were those that affected parks all over the country: the Home Guard used the open space, and the government's 'Holidays at Home' campaign provided entertainment for young people.

Holidays at Home

By 1941 there was growing pressure on the war cabinet for a national campaign to keep people at home during the holidays, the main aims being to conserve fuel supplies and save space on trains for troops. To this end local authorities were encouraged to draw up programmes of amusements for both adults and children in their parks for the summer months.

At the first meeting of Brighouse Council's Summer Holidays for Workers Sub-Committee on 17 July 1941, a suggested schedule of entertainments for Wellholme Park and the Stray was considered and approved. This was to take place from 26th July to 3rd August, and from 9th to 23rd August. £230 was allocated for costs. The borough engineer was 'instructed to make arrangements for the erection of platforms at both venues.

The *Brighouse and Elland Echo* of 22nd August has an enthusiastic review of the successful enterprise. We are told that 'the Stray has been more regularly visited by large numbers than probably at any time in its history.' The 'big crowds' were 'delighted' at the dancing displays of Rowena Ives's young performers and by the Elwyn School of Dancing. The Huddersfield Home Guard Band gave concerts, there were displays of 'drill, physical training, etc.' by local groups of boy scouts and Army Training Corps. Praise was lavished on the M.C., 'the indefatigable and versatile Will Crossley', who was 'the delight of thousands, adults as well as children'.

The following year Lane Head recreation ground became an additional venue and programmes for four weeks, from 25th July, were arranged for the three parks. A sum of £22 was allocated for the provision of folding doors to one side of the Stray shelter to form a dressing room and store room. The committee also allowed a Mrs. Watson 'to use the Stray for the Juvenile Roundabout and set of Swing boats for the holiday period only'.

The mayor of Brighouse, former Hipperholme councillor Alderman Herbert Womersley (*right*), said he 'hoped that by their arrangements they would have done something to lighten the days of war.' He asked people to support the efforts that had gone into preparing the programme of events, for which they had allocated £300, and to take their holidays at home rather than travel to resorts. 'There was no need for anyone to go to Blackpool: he had not been, and he was not going.'

(Herbert Womersley was mayor of Brighouse from 1940-42. This image, in which he wears his ceremonial robes and chain of office, was kindly supplied by his granddaughter, Elizabeth Swallow.)

John Millington, a Lightcliffe schoolboy at the time, living on Mountfields, has a clear recollection of the Stray entertainments during these summers. The stage was erected on the eastern side of the shelter and benches were placed up the hillside. He particularly remembers the M.C. encouraging them to sing a song which, according to the *Echo*, Will Crossley had written and taught to the children at the Wellholme Park and Stray concerts.

> We'll have a holiday at Brighouse,
> We'll have a holiday at home.
> Digging in the sand,
> Riding on the train,
> Going to the Stray and to Wellholme Park once again.

We'll have a holiday at Brighouse,
We'll take Mr. Womersley's advice,
Dancing to the band,
The music is so grand,
We'll have a holiday at home.

The reference to sand and the train apply only to Wellholme Park, where there was 'a large sand pit … donkey rides and trips on the miniature railway'.

In 1943, although this was in May, before the Holidays at Home weeks, the town clerk reported to the Parks Committee that he had 'on the authority of the Chairman granted permission to Mrs. Watson to place her swings and roundabouts on the Stray … the charge for the privilege being £1.' However, there was not unanimous local support for Mrs. Watson's venture. Councillor Plews reported that 'many of the residents of Hipperholme and Lightcliffe had asked by whose authority the swings, roundabouts and caravan had been set up … and some of the donors were under the impression that no show, exhibition or musical festival for which a fixed charge could be made was permissible under any circumstances, and no caravan or sleeping accommodation such as tents were allowed except by special permission of the Council.' As we have seen, there were, and presumably still are, thirty-six by-laws governing conduct on the Stray (Appendix 2) and by-laws 29 and 32 would have been contravened had the town clerk, acting 'on the authority of the Chairman', not given permission to Mrs. Watson. In any case, the meeting resolved that 'the action of the Chairman and Town Clerk in granting these applications be approved.'

In the same year there are detailed accounts of the programme for Wellholme Park, but not a mention of the Stray. It seems unlikely there were no events at other venues, especially as Lane Head had been added the previous year. Perhaps our area was a victim of the trend towards concentrating in the *Echo* on what happened in Brighouse, at the expense of peripheral villages. In his opening address at Wellholme, Alderman Womersley, now deputy mayor, did comment that, though they were 'in a happier sphere internationally', a reference to the difficulties the Germans were encountering on the Eastern Front, it was still important to avoid travel.

There is no mention of Holidays at Home in the council minutes or local newspapers of 1944. We must assume that Alderman Womersley and other residents of the Borough of Brighouse were once again free to enjoy the fresh air and fun of that little seaside town.

Home Guard

On 10 May 1940 the Germans invaded Belgium and the Netherlands, posing a threat to the shores of Britain. Four days later Anthony Eden, Secretary of State for War, made a radio broadcast in which he announced the creation of a makeshift force, to be known as Local Defence Volunteers (L.D.V.). The aim was to recruit half a million men, aged between seventeen and sixty-five, who were ineligible for regular service on account of age or reserved occupation. Within a week quarter of a million had enrolled at their local police stations; by July there were a million and a half. At the end of July their name was changed from L.D.V. (christened 'Look, Duck and Vanish' by the nation's schoolchildren) to Home Guard.[79] There followed more than four years of energy, organisation and drilling as survivors of the

First World War joined youngsters born in its aftermath to repel simulated attacks by the enemy. Eden called the movement 'a miracle of improvisation'. It was, of course, immortalised in the television series *Dad's Army*.

The Hipperholme unit was officially 'G' Company of the 22nd Battalion West Riding Home Guard, headquarters at Holly Bank, Bramley Lane. The Company Commander was Major L. Cordingley, M.C. of Linden Lea, Cecil Avenue, Sales Manager and a director of T. F. Firths'; his Second-in-Command Captain Sidney O. Shave of 16, The Crescent. The operation area took in Hipperholme, Lightcliffe, Coley, Priestley Green, Norwood Green, Hove Edge, Brookfoot and much of Southowram. There were four operational platoons, two of which appear below. 5 Platoon was obviously photographed on the Stray, 3 Platoon probably not.

3 Platoon, led by Lieut. J. F. (Jack) Pell, M.M., seated fourth from left. His deputy was Lieut. N. Walker, who I think is to Pell's left. Pell lived at 'Pic-Tor', 100, Wakefield Road, Walker at 7, The Grove.

For security reasons details of the Home Guard's manoeuvres were not publicised in local newspapers. The only reference to the Stray in the fifty-eight pages of 'G' Company's operation orders comes under the heading of 'Mined Areas', where six locations are listed as provisionally selected for mining. Three of these are on the Stray, at the north-west, south and south-east. Map references are given, but they are not Ordnance Survey co-ordinates so I can only assume they had created their own references, presumably to confuse the enemy. (The other three areas were Crow Nest Gate, Golf Course, and Upper Sutherland.)

5 Platoon, led by Lieut. G. Leo Enright (seated fourth from right). His second was Lieut. A. Mitchell.
(The bespectacled gentleman to Enright's left has an authoritarian demeanour.)
Enright lived at 23, The Crescent, Mitchell at 75, The Grove.

One ceremonial event that was reported in the *Brighouse and Elland Echo* was the fourth anniversary celebration, which took place in the early evening of Saturday, 3 November 1944.

The procession, a 'very smart parade' made up of the Home Guard, representatives from the regular army, scouts, sea scouts, Brighouse Council, and the Women's Voluntary Society (W.V.S.), assembled outside the council offices and marched along Leeds Road to a saluting base near the Congregational church.

In the photograph on the left (from the *Brighouse and Elland Echo*) are the civic representatives, led by the macebearer. Behind him are the mayor, George Bunce, and Mrs. Bunce, behind them the deputy mayor and his wife, Herbert and Ethel Womersley. The bewigged gentleman is the town clerk, Ernest Clegg.

The salute was taken by a General Cliff, Colonel Robert H. Goldthorp and the mayor, George P. Bunce, of Sunny Vale. The parade then marched to markers on the Stray, where they were addressed by General Cliff, who praised the volunteers for their war effort.

Although 'G' Company's military exercises were not covered in the local press, their socials, of which there were many, were a regular feature. One such was held on 14 March 1941 at the Conservative club (now Lightcliffe Club) overlooking the Stray. We are told that the Company 'concluded their winter programme of social activities … with a most successful whist drive and dance. The mayor and mayoress, Alderman and Mrs. H. Womersley were guests, as were the 22nd Battalion commander, Captain E. V. Blakey, and Mrs. Blakey, and Mr. C. E. Gudgin, Capt. Blakey's adjutant, and Mrs Gudgin. The *Echo* continues: 'The success of the dance was due in large measure to the excellent music by 'The Havercake Spitfires' dance band of the Duke of Wellington's Regiment, who played with great energy and enthusiasm. Paper hats and musical novelties were much appreciated by the dancers.' The mayoress presented the prizes for whist.

The country's 5,000 Home Guard companies, with 25,000 platoons, were stood down on 3 December 1944 and disbanded on 31 December 1945. The Hipperholme company formed an old comrades association. Their first function, in March 1945, attended by nearly 300, was another whist drive and dance at Lightcliffe Conservative club.

Football, Belgians, Bands and Others

Lightcliffe Congregational A.F.C. had been given permission to play their home games on the Stray for the 1938-39 season, but there is no record of any previous application from a local club. During the war years Lightcliffe Juniors and Lightcliffe, the latter competing in the Brighouse Football League, used the sloping pitch. In 1941 Lightcliffe Juniors shared the ground with the Service of Youth Council, playing alternate Saturdays.[80] Not all applications were granted. The West Riding Police (Halifax Division) wanted to play three matches in 1941, but they were given options of three other venues. Three years later the Royal Engineers were sent to Lane Head, 'provided their fixtures did not clash with those of the R.A.S.C.'

The Royal Army Service Corps, the Royal Logistic Corps since 1965, was the unit responsible for keeping the British Army supplied with all provisions except weaponry and ammunition (the responsibility of the Royal Army Ordnance Corps). In 1944 their 1016 Company was stationed in Lightcliffe as part of the build-up for D-Day. These were Belgians who had been members of the resistance movement in their country. When Belgium was liberated in September 1944, a number of young men joined the British Army. They were billeted in large empty houses such as Cliffe Hill, and The Manse on Upper Sutherland Road. Troutbeck House on Bramley Lane, without hot water or heating, housed about 100.

John Millington remembers them well. Their vehicles were parked along almost the whole length of Bramley Lane. Each day the soldiers cleaned these trucks, and painted the nuts of the wheel hubs in alternate colours. John was mystified as to the apparent pointlessness of these repeated activities until, he wryly observes, he did his national service in the 1950s. They also marched up and down Bramley Lane, and 'played at being soldiers in the fields around Priestley Green.' As John says, he and his young friends 'had a ringside seat'. His parents befriended three of the soldiers, invited them to their house every evening for food, warmth and a hot bath. John corresponded with one of them after the war.

The community obviously welcomed the Belgian soldiers of the R.A.S.C. to Lightcliffe. They played football on the Stray on Saturdays, Tuesday and Thursdays, when the pitch was not being used by other teams. Also, Saturday night dances were organised for them at the Conservative club. John Millington's notes for a talk entitled 'The Village at War' contain the comment 'Girls on Stray after dances!'[81] Presumably the post of park ranger was redundant by this time, or perhaps a blind eye was turned to the Belgian boys in khaki.

One night in March 1945, recalls John, they disappeared, went home to Belgium to spend the last weeks of the war as transport drivers. However, many of them returned more than thirty years later, in July 1977. Joan Hopwood, whose parents had taken in some of the Belgians during the war at their Upper Sutherland Road house, heard they intended to hold a ceremony at the Stray memorial on Saturday morning. She went to see them, met the president of their Verbroedering (literally, 'reconcilement, fraternisation'), Jaak Ghelen, and the secretary, Pol Steyls, who said they intended to return the following year in greater numbers. Joan and her husband, Norman, decided to organise a

programme of events, including a dance at the Conservative club, and the Lightcliffe Belgian Society was formed, Norman the chair, Joan the secretary. A close bond was established and the organisations met regularly, visiting each other's countries on alternate years. The Hopwoods' sons are still in contact with descendants of some of the Belgian soldiers who, as young men, made a brief impact on village life in the winter of 1944-45.

The Verbroedering presented the third plaque on the memorial, visible above.

The photograph above was taken during the Belgians' visit of summer 1984. At the front, from the left, are Jaak Ghelen, Councillor John Bradley, the mayor of Calderdale, and Norman Hopwood. Behind them, Joe Dresser is the Verbroedering treasurer and flag bearer, Pol Steyls the third man to his left. Mrs. Bradley, the mayoress, is to his left, then Joan Hopwood. The Rev. Hugh Neems, of Lightcliffe Congregational church, is next to the end on the right, John Millington partially obscured by him. The gentleman in spectacles at the back, behind and slightly to the left of Joan Hopwood, is Ferdinand van der Rijke.

The Verbroedering at the cenotaph in July 1989 (left).

John Millington is holding the union flag, Joe Dresser again the Belgian standard bearer. The gentleman in the light jacket could be the Belgian consul for this area, who attended one gathering. To his left is Ferdinand van der Rijke.

(Chris Helme Collection)

In June 1943 the Council granted two applications for use of the Stray by local churches, as the Wesleyans of Hipperholme and the Congregationalists of Lightcliffe unknowingly heralded their Christ Church union of 60 years later. The members of the respective Sunday schools met in the park on the afternoon of Whit Monday. A more ambitious idea was the subject of an application to the Parks Committee by the Congregational minister, the Rev. Gordon P. Smailes. He and the Rev. Bert Wright of Hipperholme sought permission to hold a Christian Forum, taking the form of a brief address followed by questions, on the Stray every Saturday evening from 8 p.m. to 9 p.m. This was granted. The forum would have long disbanded by the time the dances in the nearby Conservative club ended, avoiding any clash of interests.

Band concerts do not appear to have been held as frequently during the war years, although the Council was keen to promote and encourage performances. When the Royal Engineers gave a concert in October 1941, it was realised that there was little time for publicity, so the committee instructed the borough engineer to have posters printed, to be displayed on small notice boards on the Stray and in Hipperholme shop windows. Following V.E. Day in May 1945, an extra day's holiday was held on Monday, 2nd July. The Council decided to invite Brighouse and Rastrick, Black Dyke or the Halifax Home Guard Band to give a concert on either the Stray or Wellhome Park.

V.E. 3-Day was dull and cloudy, with a threat of rain, so that 'raincoats were carried by most people'. The Brighouse and Rastrick Band (conducted by Mr. F. Berry) and the Halifax Home Guard Band (under the baton of Mr. T. Casson) gave concerts of popular music at both Wellholme Park and the Stray. The *Echo* informs us that there were 'only comparatively small attendances, but the programmes were much appreciated nevertheless.'

It must have been anticipated that there would be an upsurge in band concerts in Brighouse's parks. In May 1945, perhaps in the optimistic wake of D-Day, the Parks and Cemeteries Committee 'considered the question of engaging Bands for giving Sunday concerts in the Council's Parks.' The following was resolved:

1) That applications be invited from first-class Bands by advertising in the next issue of "The Bandsman" for the terms on which the Bands are prepared to give Sunday performances in the Council's Parks.

2) That when a Band has been engaged the Band shall deposit the sum of £1.1s.0d. [one guinea in old money] with the Council as a guarantee that the concert will be held, this amount being returned to the Band provided the concert is held.

3) That collection sheets be placed at the entrances to the Parks and the proceeds of the collections be retained by the Council.

4) That a charge of 3d. per session be made to members of the public for the hire of the bandstand chairs [this would apply to Wellhome rather than the Stray], the proceeds of the hire of such chairs to be retained by the Council.

5) That the Summer Entertainments Sub-Committee … be requested to suggest what arrangements can be made for providing cover for the Bands who give concerts on the Stray at Lightcliffe.

(Brighouse & Elland Echo)

On 16 August 1942 the women's section of the Hipperholme and Lightcliffe Branch of the British Legion dedicated their new standard at the Stray. The ceremony was performed by the Rev. E. Parry, vicar of Coley. Also on the platform was the Rev. R. Machon, vicar of St. Thomas's, Claremount, the British Legion chaplain.

(The shelter is top left, behind the stage.)

A more unusual request came from local greengrocer Albert Hall, who sought permission to graze his horse on the Stray for a few hours each day. This was approved. Mr. Hall, a Falstaffian character, delivered fruit, vegetables and geniality by horse and cart from his wooden shop, which stood between the road and the railway line on St. Giles Road opposite Ivy Crescent, between Mayroyde and Sunnyleigh. There is a detached house on the site now. By the mid-1950s his horse and cart had given way to an ancient motor vehicle.

At the committee's October 1944 meeting the town clerk 'submitted a letter … from Mrs. Athellina W. Riley, daughter of Mrs. F. E. Wakefield, intimating her desire to give a seat on the Stray … for the use of elderly people, in remembrance of her mother.' This was agreed. It will be recalled that Frances Emma Wakefield was chair of the Ladies' Shelter Committee which had raised the funds to provide the facility in 1925. As a J.P. Mrs. Wakefield, of 7, Lane Ends Terrace, Hipperholme, was the first woman, in August 1921, to take her place on the Halifax bench. She had died earlier that year at her daughter's Frizinghall home.

Upkeep

In war as in peacetime the routine tasks of maintaining the Stray had to be carried out. Wilfred Iredale was still employed as a gardener, and probably Jim Hudson as well, so the shrubs and borders around the memorial and the toilets would be in good condition. When the edges of the paths were reported as cracking in January 1941, the committee, constrained by the necessity of making economies, could only decide to reconsider when submitting estimates for the following year. However, in early 1942 there was sufficient money to install lighting units in the toilets, and the locking at nights could be discontinued. Mr. Iredale would carry on cleaning the premises.

Mowing the Stray's eleven acres was still contracted out. In May 1942 J. L. Tankard of Norwood Green had been granted permission by the committee chairman to cut and remove the grass for use as silage, provided the grounds were left in reasonable condition. The committee ratified this decision. Three years later A. Lister of Pond Farm, Hove Edge submitted a price for mowing, and cleaning up afterwards. He proposed six shillings an hour for mowing by 'one man, horse and machine' and five shillings an hour for 'cleaning up' by 'one man, horse and cart', with half a crown an hour for 'additional labour'. This was accepted, on condition that the hourly rate for 'cleaning up' be reduced to 3s.9d. Mr. Lister agreed.

THE MEMORIAL

The memorial at about this time. Note the closely cropped grass and artistically manicured shrubs.

(John Illingworth Collection)

The May 1943 meeting of the Parks and Cemeteries Committee received a report from the superintendent of police about damage to windows and seating in the Stray shelter, caused by five youths. The borough engineer estimated the cost of repair at £6.2s.0d. The town clerk was authorised to commence legal proceedings. The case was heard at the Brighouse petty sessions on 23rd June. Unfortunately, the microfiche report of the hearing is largely illegible. I can make out the names of the five youths (and recognise some of these) and see that arrests were made by War Reserve Constable Moss. Some or all of them were in the Army Cadets or the Home Guard. Major A. Mabbott, in charge of the Army Cadets, spoke on behalf of some of them. (I can't make this out but two of them might have pleaded not guilty.) It seems (again, I can't be sure) that, after Mabbott's testimony as to previous good character, the summonses, brought under the Probation of Offenders Act 1907, were overturned on the understanding that the costs of repair were met by the youths.

Councillor Edward Alfred Oxberry lived close to the Stray, at 15, Westfield. He clearly kept an eye on its facilities, so was able to report to the committee in July 1944 that the slide and swings were in need of repair. The borough engineer confirmed two months later that the slide had been removed. At the same meeting Oxberry requested the provision of a drinking fountain, which the water engineer was authorised to provide. In May 1945 Oxberry pointed out that no start had been made on the repair of the swings, and the drinking fountain had not appeared. The borough engineer promised to see to the swings before Whitsuntide and the drinking fountain as soon as possible.

CHAPTER 8 # NEVER HAD IT SO GOOD

THE TWENTY YEARS, possibly slightly longer, following the Second World War were arguably the period during which the Stray was at its best, or perhaps I am influenced by the fact that for many of these years the Stray was my playground. There were full-time gardeners, and even extras in the summer months as, certainly from the late 1950s, students were employed. They were proud of their park: the colourful memorial gardens were carefully tended, trees were flourishing, the shelter and toilets were kept in repair, and the swings and other equipment were an attraction the whole year round.

Upkeep

In March 1946 A. Lister of Pond Farm reported that he was prepared to purchase a new machine, and quoted prices of, for mowing (one man, horse and machine) 6s. per hour; for carting and cleaning up (one man, horse and cart) 4s.6d. per hour. These terms were accepted. However, two months later the assistant parks superintendent and cemetery registrar reported that 'when Mr. A. Lister … commenced to mow the grass … he was faced with considerable difficulty, and it was apparent that the usual methods of working would not restore the Stray to good condition.' To avoid ploughing up and reseeding, the officer experimented with a gang-mower drawn by a motor-lorry. This proved successful, whereupon the committee decided to dispense with the services of Mr. Lister in favour of hiring mechanical labour, at 10s. an hour, to draw the gang-mower. The officer further reported that 'the increased cost of mechanical labour was offset by the expeditious way in which the mowing had been done; that almost all the Stray had now been cut, and that by using this method approximately every ten to fourteen days, the Stray would be restored to its pre-war condition.'

Wicksteed of Kettering supplied a new thirty-foot slide in 1947, but Councillor Oxberry's drinking fountain had still not been installed.[82] The borough engineer made enquiries, and the following month reported that the fountain ordered for the Stray had been erected at Lane Head. He had another in stock and would ensure this was in place as soon as possible. He was as good as his word, although it evidently caused occasional problems, and from time to time the water engineer was instructed to carry out necessary repairs. On one occasion there was a burst service pipe, but I can confirm that the fountain worked well for several years from the mid-fifties.

Brighouse Council covered a significantly larger area than Hipperholme U.D.C. but there was still the occasional impression of a close liaison between officials and gardeners. Matters which would eventually be unrecorded or temporarily ignored were documented in the committee minutes. In January 1947 attention was drawn to the state of two large trees, a Dutch elm near the entrance to the railway station and an ash opposite the Conservative club. The elm was to be removed, for reasons of public safety, but for the time being, the ash remained. (It is no longer there.) The following month a strip of turf ten feet wide, 'rising steeply to the War Memorial', was removed to the King George V Park, and a flower border made in its place. In the autumn of the following year the parks superintendent was 'required to add colour to the grass verge … along Whitehall Road next spring, as he considers most advisable.' He undertook to plant crocuses and daffodils along that section, and around the memorial.

A summer morning in about 1950, clouds gathering.   (John Illingworth Collection)

In 1950 the parks superintendent reported that it would not be possible to repair the paths on the Stray owing to a shortage of labour. Perhaps there was an interregnum brought about by the retirements of Messrs. Iredale and Hudson. Mr. A. Hodgson of Pond House, Smithy Carr Lane was therefore engaged on the same terms as those agreed between him and the highways department for road and footpath repairs.

Vandalism was an occasional problem, usually to the windows of the shelter, occasionally to trees. In April 1953 a Parks Committee minute entitled 'Vandalism, etc. at the Stray' read as follows:

> 'The Parks Superintendent in his monthly report referred to the damage occasioned to shrubs, plants and flowering cherry trees due to the playing of football in parts of the Stray away from the football pitch; to the alleged infringement of the Byelaw prohibiting cycling in pleasure grounds; and to the persistent breaking of glass in the public shelter on the Stray.
> Resolved: (a) That the Town Clerk be instructed to request the co-operation of the Headmaster of the school now referred to [Lightcliffe Primary?] regarding infringements of the Byelaw prohibiting cycling in pleasure grounds, and (b) that the Police be informed of the damage to the public shelter on the Stray, and that they be requested to take appropriate steps to obviate further vandalism of this nature.'

At the May meeting of Brighouse Council, Councillor Hallowell commented on the committee minute, saying that 'such damage was general in the borough.' It was the committee's policy to ask the police to prosecute when the offenders were known, although a warning would be issued in the case of minor damage to trees. On 26 August 1954 the *Courier* reported that 'a 16-year-old Lightcliffe girl was fined £1 at Brighouse Juvenile Court today for riding a pedal cycle on the Stray, contrary to the Council's bye-laws.' In June 1956 the chairman of the committee had authorised the police to proceed after receiving reports of damage to windows. Three months later the town clerk reported that 'a sum of £8.14s.0d. had been received from the Clerk to the Justices being reimbursement of compensation paid by certain boys who had caused damage to a shelter at the Stray.'

The 4th of November, the eve of Bonfire Night, was Mischief Night.[83] At the Brighouse Council's meeting of 5 December 1960, the chairman of the Parks and Cemeteries Committee, Councillor J. K. Pickard, asked 'When is this anticipation of 5 November going to be banned entirely by the law of this land?'[84] He listed damage carried out in the borough's parks, including the Stray, where 'Bottles of all kinds had been broken and widely scattered in the shelters and on the footpaths.'

The shelter windows continued to provide a problem, so in 1961 the borough engineer sought quotations for cheaper alternatives to the reinforced glass. Replacing all the windows with 5-plywood panels would cost £40; breeze blocks, finished with rough rendering £60. The committee opted for the latter, as shown in the photograph below, taken not long after the windows had been replaced.

Stray, c.1961.   *(John Illingworth Collection)*

The only other reference to vandalism during the period covered by this book occurred in 1973, when the parks superintendent reported on 'extensive vandalism during the summer months' in several of the Council's parks. Nothing was specified, and the town clerk was asked to write to Chief Inspector Frost of the West Yorkshire Constabulary requesting that special attention to these parks be given by the police in future.

There were occasional complaints from members of the public, some of them so trivial as to be laughable, or perhaps a testimony to a long-gone close relationship between a local authority and its community, depending on your point of view. In January 1947 the committee received a letter from Major J.A.S. Brooke of Netherfield (Lot 46 on the 1907 auction plan) to the effect that gardeners had prevented delivery of a load of manure across the Stray to the back of his house. He pointed out that he had a previous agreement with Hipperholme U.D.C. (which had ceased to exist ten years previously) to carry out this practice. Permission was granted to Mr. Brooke, on the understanding that 'loads are led across the Stray only when the ground is in a firm condition.' I think we can see why the gardeners objected to a vehicle crossing the Stray during the wet winter months. Joe Brooke was a brother of Newton Brooke, chairman of Hipperholme U.D.C. after the First World War, influential in the creation of the Memorial Stray.

In the summer of 1954 Edward Oxberry, now elevated to alderman, reported that he had received a complaint from a resident that seed from long grass at the edge of the Stray had blown into his garden. The resident was assured that the issue would be dealt with as soon as similar work had been completed at the Bailiff Bridge memorial garden. There is no mention of a previous agreement with Hipperholme Council that grass seed would not blow into neighbouring gardens.

There were occasional tributes to the gardeners of the Stray. In December 1950 Kenneth Wilson, of 2, Park Terrace, wrote to the town clerk 'expressing the thanks of local residents for the splendid treatment of the Stray during the past summer.' Mr. Wilson went further, when he suggested 'the thinning out of the ornamental shrubs bordering the diagonal paths which led to Whitehall Road, in order to expose the flower beds to public view.' The committee resolved 'That Mr. Wilson be informed that it is the policy of this committee, as circumstances permit, to carry out the substitution of existing privets and ornamental shrubs with more colourful subjects.' No thanks for the compliment he had made.

The Stray in about 1960. (John Illingworth Collection.) Brookes' chimneys in the background.

Five years later Alderman Oxberry reported that he had received 'several expressions of appreciation of the excellent condition in which the Stray … had been maintained this summer.' On this occasion praise was unequivocal.

Cricket, Football and Sledging

As a child and a youth, I played cricket on the Stray for countless summer hours. There was never any friction between us and members of the public, apart from when we occasionally needed to retrieve the ball from the gardens of Rylstone or Netherfield, and only then if we were spotted; and we were cunning. This easy relationship had evidently not always been the case. In September 1951 Mr. R. N. Fitton of Holly Bank objected to the 'playing of cricket in close proximity to the footpath leading across the Stray', a practice which was 'alleged to have caused considerable apprehension to members of the public using the Stray.' The parks superintendent was asked to take whatever action he deemed appropriate in such circumstances, which I like to think was a diplomatic way of minuting, 'Ignore this'. Five years later the town clerk reported to the committee that he had received complaints from 'residents of two houses adjacent to the Stray regarding damage which had been done to their property by youths playing cricket.' The town clerk was asked to inform the complainants that he had been instructed to report to the next meeting of the committee 'on the possibility of Byelaws being made prohibiting the playing of games by persons over the age of sixteen years.'

In the mid-to-late 1950s there was a cricket team called Stray Gents. This was set up and organised by Gareth Lewis, elder son of the St. Matthew's curate, Rev. W. D. Lewis.[85] The family lived close to the Stray, on Westfield, four doors from Alderman Oxberry.[86]

Stray Gents, c. 1957. Back row, l to r: Chris Moss, Stuart West, Robert Brooke, David Shaw, Colin Helliwell, Philip Webb. Front row: David 'Lana' Turner, Michael Shaw, Gareth Lewis, Chris Webb, John Whitley, Paul Martin.
Also: Stuart Sugden, Mick Wright, Dave Houston, Malcolm Wade, and others.

Almost sixty years later Chris Webb remembers their games with affection. He tells me that the main opposition was provided by Hipperholme Methodists, organised by David Robinson and including Brian Wade, Graham Haigh, Andrew Mattingley and others. Members of both teams knew each other through school, in most cases either Hipperholme or Whitcliffe Mount grammar schools. On one occasion Peter Edmondson, a Hipperholme contemporary of Paul Martin, brought a team who played a two-innings match over a whole day in the summer holiday of 1957. Their ground was the area bounded on three sides by Leeds Road, the avenue of limes between the memorial and shelter, and the long wall at the side of Holly Grove. Joan Milner and her friend, Julie Isaacs, were supporters, Joan irreverently referring to the team as 'Lightcliffe Louts'. She later married one of the players, Stuart Sugden, great great grandson of Thomas Sugden, founder of the flour milling business.

From the late 1940s the Stray football pitch was the domain of Hipperholme United Juniors. Their name first appears in council minutes in 1948, when the Brighouse Youth Football League applied on their behalf for use of the Stray every Saturday afternoon. As their members became senior players, they obtained sponsorship from a Shelf business and entered the Halifax Football League as Reynolds Rangers. The photograph below is Reynolds Rangers Juniors in their final season of 1955-56. Nev Lunn, a skilful inside forward, remembers his team as Hipperholme United Juniors, playing in kit handed on by Reynolds Rangers, but the list of teams which appeared on Friday evenings in the *Halifax Courier* has them as 'Reynolds Rangers Juniors'.

Reynolds Rangers, in their final season before changing their name to Hipperholme United. Back row, left to right: Leslie Howe (manager), John Clough, Geoff Howe, Alan Sykes, Brian Barron, Philip Lumb, Bill Curran. Front row: Brian Dodding, Neville Lunn, Graham Normington, Ian Simpson, Neville Lumb. (David Curran Collection)

The 1948 council minute refers to the fact that there was a need for changing facilities on the Stray. Both the team photographs here were taken in the grounds of Lydgate House, in front of an archway which led to the kitchen garden, the Stray beyond. The players changed in a barn across the yard from the main building. There have never been changing rooms on the Stray.

(Lightcliffe & District Local History Society Collection)

In 1956-57 they were Hipperholme United, no longer juniors, resplendent in smart black-and-white striped shirts. They were a smart team too. The Halifax League had nine or ten divisions in those days and my recollection is of a number of successive promotions. I haven't checked this in case a fond childhood memory is shattered. They certainly won something in the first season under their new name, as the photograph below confirms.

Hipperholme United, 1956-57. Back row, left to right: Leslie Howe (manager), Gary Boothroyd, Neville Lunn, Alan Sykes, Arthur Watts, Jack Wray, Bill Curran. Front row: Raymond Richardson, Neville Lumb, Geoff Howe, Brian Dodding, Brian Barron, Keith Mallinson.   *(David Curran Collection)*

Reynolds Rangers was not the only team to play at the Stray in the early 1950s. A *Courier* article of 22 October 1952 reports a notification to the Halifax Football Association that 'Stoney Lane dress at White Horse Inn and play at the Stray, Lightcliffe.'

Lightcliffe primary school played games on the full-sized football pitch, although twenty-two small boys found it difficult to make effective use of such a large area. The school also held games lessons there when their field was being reseeded in the early 1960s, after which football matches were sensibly transferred to the smaller school pitch. Lightcliffe High School, situated in the former Liberal club, mentioned in the 1907 auction, also held lessons in the park. With the advent of Sunday football in the 1970s, Hare and Hounds Athletic used the Stray as their home ground. Hipperholme Methodists Under 16s, of the Halifax Junior League, were there for a few years around 1960, and there were many games organised between rival groups of youngsters, as well as impromptu matches involving whoever turned up on winter weekends or school holidays. From the mid-1970s there was an annual boy scout and wolf cub football tournament.

In winters there was a time when the Stray could be covered in snow for weeks; sometimes even longer, as in 1946-47 and 1962-63. Football gave way to sledging, snowball fights, the building of gigantic 'barricades', as children from the village's four corners shared the thrills of the slope behind the shelters. Action would begin soon after first light and continue until well into the dark of the evening. The area at the top became iced over so that you had to edge along the Friars Crag wall with your sledge before descending, seeing how far you could slide, across the path, towards the cherry trees or Holgate's oaks, into untouched snow. Yorkshireman J. B. Priestley understood: 'The first fall of snow is not only an event but it is a magical event. You go to bed in one kind of world and wake up to find yourself in another quite different, and if this is not enchantment, where is it to be found?'[87] The Stray was transformed: summer cricket, the swings, hide-and-seek games forgotten as we entered the portal of a silent, white, changed world. Magical days indeed.

Sledging in 1958. In the centre foreground are Nigel Denham, grandson of Algernon, and Rose Pickles (née Brown). To Rose's left is Libby Brearley, while to her right and behind, in apparent difficulties, is her brother, Chris. Katherine Bunney is the girl with the pigtails on the left.
(Rose Pickles Collection)

A recent photograph, so no shelter, but a good illustration of the enduring popularity of the Stray as a winter playground. *(Dave Lister Collection)*

I have mentioned what were known collectively as 'the swings'. On page 71 is a photograph of the slide and two sets of swings, and a 'rant' similar to the one on the Stray. However, two vital pieces of equipment have defied all attempts to obtain images, apart from the one to the left. These are the 'monkey climb', and the structure below the 'rant': a set of gymnastic equipment comprising a rope, ladder, horizontal bar, rings, and trapeze. The monkey climb was a horizontal ladder situated between the 'grown-up' swings and the 'rant', about six feet from the ground, metal supports at both ends and in the middle, with two rungs at one end to make it possible to climb. You could walk (very risky) or crawl along the top or swing from the rungs, Tarzan-like, until your arms found the strain too great. Monkey climb, rant and gymnastic equipment disappeared about fifty years ago, presumably designated 'potentially dangerous' by a committee of adults in faraway Halifax.

Linda King climbs the ladder in 1962, with the assistance of a friend.

(David and Sheila Fitton Collection)

Bands and Methodists

The era of the Sunday afternoon brass band concert in public parks survived into the 1950s when, on the Stray as elsewhere, fashions changed, due at least partly to increasing ownership of television and family cars. In 1946 there were only two concerts, but the importance of these to the local authority is evident from a minute of the Parks Committee meeting of April 1946.

> 'The Town Clerk reported that he had endeavoured to make arrangements for the use of the following premises in the event of unfavourable weather for the two Band Concerts arranged in the Stray:
>
>> The Hipperholme and Lightcliffe Conservative Club,
>> Bramley Lane Congregational School,
>> The top floor of the Lightcliffe Liberal Club, and
>> The Hipperholme Wesleyan Church Sunday School,
>
> but all the said premises were either unavailable or unsuitable for the purpose.
>
> Resolved: That in the event of unfavourable weather the two Band Concerts … be held in the Savoy Cinema, Brighouse …'

The extent to which Brighouse Council was prepared to assist the bands can only reflect the value placed on these events.

However, the Last Post was not far away. The only further reference to brass bands on the Stray occurs in 1952, when the 'Clifton and Lightcliffe Subscription Band' was granted permission to hold concerts on 18th May, 15th June and 3rd August.

The brass band movement continues to flourish, if with a smaller number of bands than in its Victorian and Edwardian heyday, even if regular open air concerts are regrettably a feature of local life which came to an end more than half a century ago. However, at the same time as these performances ended, an interest in the open spaces of the Stray arose up the road at the Hipperholme Methodist Sunday school. In 1954 the secretary of their council applied for permission to hold a 'Scholars' Field Day' on Saturday, 19th June, using forms and tables 'as it is intended to provide tea for the scholars'. Permission was forthcoming, and similar applications were made in most years of the following decade. In 1958 the forms and tables were requested 'to mark out a section for races.' At least one of the scholars of those days recalls tables laden with buns, but has no recollection of the exertions which were a preliminary to the feasting.

Remembrance

The *Halifax Courier* of Monday, 20 September 1948 contained an account of the local branch of the British Legion's annual drumhead and memorial service, held the previous day.[88] A parade of ex-servicemen and council officials marched along Leeds Road from Hipperholme to the Stray for a service, taken by St. Matthew's vicar Canon H. L. Taylor, at the war memorial. Prayers were led by his curate, C. F. Goodchild, and the lesson was read by the Rev. P. Dolphin of Lightcliffe Congregational church.

The ceremony accompanying the unveiling of a memorial plaque in memory of those whose lives were lost in the Second World War was performed by Alderman Wilfred Whiteley, mayor of Brighouse. This was identical in style and lettering to the First World War memorial. Col. R. H. Goldthorp unveiled the roll of honour, and Canon Taylor dedicated the plaque. A concluding address was given by the Rev. I. Clark, vicar of Coley.

Inscriptions on the Stray war memorial (left), commemorating the villagers of Hipperholme, Lightcliffe and Bailiff Bridge who lost their lives in the two world wars. The plaque at the top was presented by the Belgian veterans who, as young men, had been stationed in Lightcliffe in 1944-45. (Author's Collection)

The Stray was, of course, the Memorial Stray. If awareness of its origin had weakened over the years, this was perhaps inevitable as younger people, born long after the First World War, enjoyed its facilities. However, on one Sunday every year the Stray was, and is, the venue for a remembrance day parade and service. As the photograph below of the 1956 service *(courtesy of Chris Helme)* shows, this was attended by members of the British Legion, veterans of both world wars, civic dignitaries, the Lightcliffe wolf cub pack, local men, many of whom, in this 1956 photograph, would have been veterans of both world wars, and curious young people.   *(Details overleaf.)*

The lowered flag is held by Edgar Clay, flanked, to his left, by his brother Walter. I think the gentleman to his right is Mr. Derbyshire, who lived on Ivy Terrace, St. Giles Road. Behind them the civic party are, front row left to right: the Mayor, Alderman Harry Edwards; Mayoress Mrs. Liza Edwards (my first teacher at Lightcliffe primary school); Deputy Mayoress Mrs. Hume. Behind them is Deputy Mayor Leslie Hume, wearing his chain of office. The three men in line with him could be Brighouse councillors. Of the men standing at the back, the one on the extreme right is Ron Hawtin, regional secretary of the British Legion. He and his family lived at Hill Top, St. Giles Road. Moving to the left, the bald man at the back could be Sam Briggs, who has made an earlier appearance in the book in connection with the Clifton and Lightcliffe Band, while the tallest gentleman is Harold West. The gentleman immediately to the right of the shrubs looks like Edward Oxberry. The wolf cub in the centre of the photograph, who has respectfully removed his cap, is the author, aged eight years. I should know my fellow wolf cubs but, apart from Geoffrey Richardson behind me on the right, names have gone, though faces remain.

CHAPTER 9

SILVER JUBILEE GALA 1977

NORMAN LISTER, Head of Lightcliffe primary school, wrote an introduction to the programme. He suggested that there would be many people around who remembered the last silver jubilee, that of George V, forty-one years previously. At that time the centre of local government for our district was at Leeds Road, Hipperholme, then it moved to Brighouse, before we became 'a much smaller voice in control of our destiny' with the advent of Calderdale. Norman then looked at changes which had taken place during the twenty-five years of Elizabeth's reign.

Fields and allotments between Bramley Lane and Leeds Road had become housing. [Referring to The Drive, Astral Avenue and Astral Close.]

A council estate had been built on farmland at Stoney Lane.

There had been two new schools, at Cliffe Hill and Eastfield [the latter now Lightcliffe Academy].

Brookes' chimneys, and Brookes itself, had gone.

Lightcliffe Station, departure point for many summer holidays, had closed.

The tall buildings opposite the shops at Hipperholme had gone, as had Smallwood's farmhouse, which was now a car park.

HIPPERHOLME & LIGHTCLIFFE

QUEEN'S JUBILEE
GALA

in aid of Christian Aid
and the Queen's Jubilee Appeal

SOUVENIR PROGRAMME

SATURDAY 14th MAY 1977

Assemble 1·15pm
Procession leaves Smith House Lane at 1·30pm
arriving at

THE STRAY

at 2·30pm (approx.)

Admission by Programme:–

10p

(The 'tall buildings')　　　　　　('Smallwood's' Farm, 'tall buildings' behind)

(Both photographs John Illingworth Collection)

The former football pitch opposite Smallwood's farm had become Sandholme estate.

The fields near the Donkey bridge were now the Westfield estate.

He then looked at what was unchanged.

Local churches still exercised their ministries, 'although old Lightcliffe Church has been reduced to a tower.'

Schools have increased in size and number.

The Good Companions, and other organisations, continue to flourish and do good work.

Association football received a blow when Lightcliffe A.F.C. folded, but the Old Brodleians had enlarged their rugby playing area.

Golf, cricket, bowls, archery and other sports were still played.

Local inns continued to provide a 'warm and welcoming atmosphere' and were a forum for discussing 'matters of the moment'.

The Stray remained an open space, although the surrounding countryside had been 'somewhat spoiled by tall electric pylons'.

Norman concluded by saying we should 'look back with thankfulness and forward with resolution.'

A list of advertisers gives an insight into changes of the past forty-six years. The businesses of at least half of the fourteen sponsors no longer exist.

Firth's Carpets Ltd.

Shepherd's, 1 St. Giles Road – Grocers, Greens and Fruit, Bread, Bacon and Ham.

Ellis's of Wyke Ltd., Hipperholme – Continental Patissiers.

D.G. & J. Ackroyd, Lightcliffe Post Office – Newsagents, Toys, Books, Cards for all Occasions.

D. Bottomley's, Leeds Road – Colour TV Service – Seven Days a Week Service.

A.&G. Motors (prop. A. and G. Waterfall), Wakefield Road – Sales, Service, Repairs, B.L.M.C. Specialists, M.O.T. Testing Station.

Hare and Hounds – John and Barbara welcome you … Webster's Sparkling Beers. Lunches available Monday to Friday.

Arnold Albutt, 54, Wakefield Road – joiner and funeral director.

Peter Manning – Newspapers, Books, Sweets, Tobacco, Toys, Greeting Cards.

Jones' Pet Store, 7, Halifax Road – Pets and Pet Supplies, Tropical and Cold Water Fish.

Headlands Garage – Petrol, Oil, Batteries, M.O.T. Testing, New and Used Cars.

Spar, 12, Leeds Road – 'Where Good Value is Shelf Evident'.

Chas. Geo. Calvert, 46, Wakefield Road – Plumber, Glazier, Hot Water and Sanitary Engineer, Ironmongery, China and Cut Glass.

Vernon Moss Ltd., Churchfields Road, Brighouse – Electro Platers – Chromium, Nickel, Copper and Bronze.

Fearnley Farms Ltd., Denholmegate Road – Finest Quality Pork, Beef and Lamb. Frozen Meat Specialists.

Aerial view of the Stray in the mid-1970s. Park Close in the foreground, Lydgate House almost obscured by autumn trees, football match in progress. *(Lightcliffe & District Local History Society Collection)*

The programme contained a list of 'Acknowledgements', which appears below.

Mr. G. Denney	Mr. I. C. Selkirk
Mr. J. Kerrin	Mr. C. J. Wood
Mr. K. G. Walls	Mrs. A. Smailes
Mrs. Hamer	Mr. G. Woodhead
Hipperholme Methodist Church	Lightcliffe St. Matthew's Church
Coley Church	United Reform Church
Hipperholme & Lightcliffe Community Council	Hipperholme Infants' School
Hipperholme Grammar School	Old Brodleians
Hipperholme & Lightcliffe Conservative Club	Lightcliffe Cubs & Scouts
Hipperholme & Lightcliffe Conservative Assoc.	Hipperholme Good Companions
Lightcliffe C. of E. School	Eastfield School
Townswomen's Guild	Calderdale
Brighouse West Riding Police	Hare & Hounds Athletic
G.K.N. Drive Line (Sponsors of 5-a-Side)	Hare & Hounds
Ryburn School Band	British Legion Band
Streak Freaks (Cars)	Morris Dancers
Firth Carpets	Brighouse Echo
Calvert (Plumbers)	Bottomley's T.V.
Phillips Domestic Appliances	Mrs. Jagger (Fortune Teller)
A.&G. Motors	Ackroyd Newsagents
Manning's Newsagent	Albutt, Joiner
Ellis, Confectioners	Headlands Garage
Fearnley Farms	Jones' Pet Stores
Shepherd's, Off-Licence	Vernon Moss
Bassan Spar Shop	Pettrick's, Newsagents
Geoff Allen (Butcher)	Venture Scouts
St. John Ambulance Brigade	Mr. R. N. Lister
Mr. & Mrs. J. B. Widdop (Caravan)	Dr. J. Lawson
Mr. S. Goodson	Miss Rosa-Lyn Kay
Sergeant Harrison	Mr. S. J. Atkinson
Mr. E. R. Lawson	Mr. R. Mitchell
Mr. D. Hey	Mrs. L. Salkeld

The *Echo* report of the gala begins by suggesting the organising committee was hoping for 2,000 visitors; in the event, there were almost 3,000, despite the Stray having been 'soaked by the previous day's rain'. Chairman Gordon Denney was 'overwhelmed by the response', adding 'the co-operation all round Hipperholme and Lightcliffe was marvellous.'

The event began at 1.30 p.m. with a procession. This gathered at the junction of Smith House Lane and Wakefield Road, at the top of the hill above Bailiff Bridge. It followed Wakefield Road to Hipperholme, encircled the Sandholme estate before retracing part of its route and turning left along Sutherland Road.

Participants were the Brighouse British Legion Band, entrants in the fancy dress and decorated bicycle competitions, the Lightcliffe Scout Band, and members of the Street Freaks custom car group. 'Gala Queen Helen Denney and her two attendants, Rachel Blamires and Donna Murray, rode in an open-topped Chevrolet car provided by the Street Freaks.' All the local churches had floats, and the procession was joined by their respective ministers: Rev. Frank Drinkwater, Vicar of Coley, Rev. Hugh Neems, Minister of Lightcliffe United Reformed Church, and the Rev. E. W. Guthrie Burgess, minister of Hipperholme Methodist Church.

Awaiting the arrival of the procession.   *(Chris Helme Collection)*

Helen Denney and Donna Murray in the Chevrolet.   *(Helen Denney Collection.)*

Stalls were organised as follows:

Hipperholme Methodist Church – grocery and white elephant;
St. John's Church, Coley – bottles and gifts;
Hare & Hounds Athletic – 'housey-mousey' [housey-mousey?];
St. Matthew's – crockery smashing and tombola;
Scouts Venture Unit – 'roll a penny';
Huddersfield Army Youth – rifle range;
Good Companions – cakes;
Old Brodleians – coconut shy;
Lightcliffe Scout Group – darts;
Methodist Games Group – target game;
Congregational Players – jubilee balloons
Hipperholme & Lightcliffe Community Association – plants;
Hipperholme & Lightcliffe Young Wives & Conservative   Association – books

Above left is Gala Queen Helen Denney (From Helen's Collection.). On the right is Helen again, with her attendant, Donna Murray. Alan Dowson is on Helen's right, Geoff Middleton to the left of Donna. The flag bearers are the Smailes twins, Paul on the left of the photo, Adrian on the right. Ian McDonald is behind Paul. The scout leader at the back is Stuart Cotterill. (The Smailes twins are the grandsons of Gordon Smailes, former minister of Lightcliffe Congregational church.)

Fancy Dress Competition.   *(Chris Helme Collection.)*

Displays were given by children from Hipperholme Infants' School, who performed maypole dances; there were Latvian Dancers, and the Lightcliffe C. of E. School country dancing and gymnastic group. There were performances by the Ryburn School Band and the Royal British Legion Band. There was also a fairground organ, fortune-teller, and puppet and magic shows. Whitehall Rovers won the five-a-side football, defeating Bailiff Bridge Cubs 2-1 in the final. The winners of the fancy dress, judged by Lightcliffe parish church assistant priest, Rev. Stanley Whitcombe and Mrs. Whitcombe, were Francesca and Emmerson Montgomery, Kirsten Thornton, and Anthony Smith. Christopher Megson won the decorated bicycle contest. In the tug o' war final the Old Brodleians powered their way to victory over Hipperholme Methodist church.

Lightcliffe councillor, later local M.P., Donald Thompson praised the gala organisers for the way they cleaned up the Stray after the event. "By 9 p.m. there wasn't a single piece of waste paper to be seen … They did a fantastic job …" Gordon Denney and the committee were 'very, very pleased.' The event raised £1,000, shared between the Queen's Silver Jubilee Appeal and Christian Aid.

EPILOGUE

I was brought up on Park Terrace, the first row of houses above what was then the Conservative club. The gardens were open plan. From our front door at number 3, I ran diagonally across Wilson's lawn at 2, Trigg's at number 1, hopped over the wall in the corner, crossed Wakefield Road, a quiet thoroughfare in those days, and I was on the Stray. There was a notice board, with a list of things I couldn't do, and an old ash tree. To my left was a wall topped by a fence, on the other side of which was Ackroyd's garden. On the right were the toilets, surrounded by shrubs, with its drinking fountain a few yards in front. Some of the trees lining the paths were well established; others were saplings. There was a clear view of the bottom goalposts if it was winter, and the shelter. The memorial was partially visible, above the avenue of lime trees.

As children we had little appreciation of the significance of the stone memorial. This wasn't because we were callous; I don't think we realised that the granite plinth embodied the whole point of the existence of our playground. On one day a year, each November, there was a parade and remembrance service, which I joined as a wolf cub in the 1950s. However, I always felt that this was an adult ceremony, and knew that it signified something profoundly tragic and sad. Writing this book has reinforced that awareness. I think of the parents, wives, sisters, brothers, lovers, of these victims, most of them youngsters whose lives were ended just as they reached adulthood. Thirty years later I knew some of their families, for whom the message they left on a floral tribute on that September afternoon in 1923 was the final word. I hope that walking in the Hipperholme and Lightcliffe Memorial Stray gave them some solace.

(Dominic Turner Collection)

APPENDIX 1   IN   MEMORIAM

1914

29 October	Thomas Daw
11 November	Frank Newsome

1915

10 March	Bruno C. Wakefield
30 April	Wilford Spencer
1 July	Fred Mitchell
25 September	Ernest Wolfenden
13 October	John A. B. Jolly
20 October	Norman Muff
31 October	Joseph A. Holt
2 December	Joseph P. Bolland
9 December	Roland Walker

1916

4 April	Walter Pybus
1 July	Harry Minnett
	Charles Newsome
2 July	Herbert Addy
9 July	Edward Schofield
11 July	Leonard Quarmby
18 July	Reginald Naylor
23 July	Harold Hoyle
17 August	Arthur Rushworth
2 September	Christopher Kershaw
3 September	Herbert Aspinall
	Frank Atack
	Austin A. Hitchin
	Horace Shaw
4 September	Aaron Sucksmith
	Bertram Wood
18 September	Thomas Stocks
3 October	Alban Borley-Mace
	Richard B. Greenwood
8 October	Joe W. Shaw
26 October	Fred Booth
16 November	Arthur C. Needham
18 November	Arthur Seed

22 November	May Hartley
24 November	Percy White
8 December	Walter Sucksmith

1917

7 January	Herbert Schofield
3 March	Willie Fielding
9 April	Herman Hardcastle
	Thomas Stocks
10 April	William H. Howe
14 April	Harry Morrist
19 April	Herbert Rhodes
25 April	Clement Baxter
29 April	Arthur Leigh
3 May	Walter H. Bucknall
	Harry S. Riley
2 June	Harold Sharp
7 June	Sam Bailey
9 June	Harry R. Spence
1 August	James Smallwood
4 August	William Harrison
27 September	George P. S. Brown
2 October	Frank Wressle
8 October	Albert E. Quarmby
9 October	Arthur V. Sternwhite
14 October	Sam Rhodes
29 October	Norris Rhodes
31 October	Sam Balmforth
17 November	Sam Lumb
26 November	Raymond Crowther
11 December	Arthur Naylor
14 December	Gerald White

1918

5 February	Reginald Pohlmann
22 March	George Turton
23 March	Edwin Dyson

27 March	Herbert Pybus
	Edgar Sharpe
12 April	Ernest Tattersfield
13 April	Rylatt Wakefield
17 April	Alfred Stubbs
20 April	Norman Hirst
	Harold Mann
23 April	John Hanson
25 April	John P. Morrison
26 April	John R. Berry
19 September	William H. Bailey
29 September	Wharton Thompson
30 September	Herbert Hoyle
2 October	Arthur T. Greaves
9 October	Benjamin Brown
12 October	Harry B. Warhurst
22 October	Walter Wolfenden
25 October	Harry Aspinall
27 October	James Wolfenden
2 November	Harold Barraclough
	Ernest Clegg
3 November	Walter Oates
6 November	Arthur D. Hemingway
9 November	Charles R. Firth
24 December	Joe Lum Brooke

1919

7 March	Robert B. Brownrigg
23 March	David G. McKeand
13 December	Milton Aspinall
Unknown	Edgar Pollard

1920

23 November	Leonard Sucksmith

1924

12 March	Ernest Wolfenden

YEAR UNKNOWN

W. Barraclough
Sam Bentley
William H. Bentley
Fred Berry
Kenneth R. Berry
Herbert Burgess
W. Cordingley
B. Greenwood
Willie Law
Thomas Moran
T. Parkinson
Edward Sutcliffe

This is a complete list of the 109 men and one woman in Hipperholme U.D.C. who lost their lives during the First World War, either in direct combat, or as a result of wounds. The woman, May Hartley, died in an accident while involved in war work at Joseph Brooke and Sons, where she was employed.

All but fifteen of the names appear on local memorials, some on more than one. Many are remembered in inscriptions at St. Matthew's Churchyard.

The concentration from I July 1916 coincides with the Battle of the Somme, that in March and April 1918 with the German Spring Offensive.

BYELAWS

Made by the HIPPERHOLME URBAN DISTRICT COUNCIL, with respect to the PLEASURE GROUND known as "The Stray."

1.   Throughout these byelaws the expression "the Council" means the URBAN DISTRICT COUNCIL OF HIPPERHOLME and the expression "the stray" means the pleasure ground known as "THE HIPPERHOLME AND LIGHTCLIFFE WAR MEMORIAL STRAY."

2.   The provisions contained in the following bylaws numbered 7, 9, 12, 13, 14, and 29 shall not be deemed to apply to any officer of the Council in the proper execution of his duty or to any person or servant of any person employed by the Council in the proper execution of any work in connexion with the laying out, planting, improvement, or maintenance of the stray.

3.   A person shall not wilfully or improperly remove or displace any board, plate, or tablet, or any support, fastening, or fitting of any board, plate, or tablet used or constructed or adapted to be used for the exhibition of any byelaw or notice, and fixed or set up by the Council in any part of the stray, or in any building or structure therein, or at or near to any one of the appointed means of entrance to or egress from the stray, or in or on any wall or fence enclosing the stray.

4.   A person shall not carelessly or negligently deface, injure, or destroy any part of any wall or fence in or enclosing the stray, or any part of any building, barrier, or railing, or any fixed or moveable seat, or any other structure or erection in the stray.

5.   A person shall not paint, write, cut, carve or in any manner inscribe letters, figures or marks upon, or otherwise disfigure any rock or tree, or any wall or fence or other structure or erection on the stray.

6.   A person shall not wilfully, carelessly, or negligently remove or displace any barrier, railing, or post, or any fixed or moveable seat, or any part of any building, structure, or erection, or any monument, work of art, ornament, or decoration, or any implement, utensil, apparatus, appliance, or article provided for use or used or adapted to be used in the laying out, planting, improvement,

or maintenance of the stray, or in the care, cultivation, or protection of any tree, sapling, shrub, Underwood, gorse, or other plant in the stray.

7. A person shall not at any time ride, drive, or bring, or cause or suffer to be ridden, driven, or brought into the stray any beast of draught or burden.

8. A person shall not drive or bring, or cause to be driven or brought into the stray any bull, ox, cow, heifer, steer, cough, sheep, lamb, hog, pig, or sow, unless, in pursuance of an agreement with the council, or otherwise in the exercise of any lawful right or privilege, such person may be duly authorised to drive or bring any such animal or to cause any such animal to be driven or brought into the stray for pasturage or for any other lawful purpose.

9. A person shall not at any time drive or wheel or cause or suffer to be driven or wheeled into the stray any barrow, truck, or machine, or any vehicle other than a wheeled chair drawn or propelled by hand, or a perambulator or a chaise drawn or propelled by hand and used solely for the conveyance of a child or children, or an invalid.

   Provided that where the council set apart any such part of the stray as may be fixed by the council and maybe described in the notice board affixed or set up in some conspicuous position in the stray, for the use of bicycles, tricycles, or other similar machines, this by law shall not be deemed to prohibit the driving or wheeling of any bicycle, tricycle, or other similar machine, in or to such part of the stray.

10. A person who shall wheel or bring, or cause to be wheeled or brought into the stray A wheeled chair drawn or propelled by hand, or a perambulator or a chaise drawn or propelled by hand and used solely for the conveyance of a child or children, or an invalid, shall not at any time wheel or station such chair, perambulator, or chaise, or cause or suffer such chair, perambulator, or chaise to be wheeled or stationed over or upon any part of a flower bed, or over or upon any tree, sapling, shrub, underwood, gorse, or other plant, or any ground in course of preparation or cultivation as a flower bed, or for the reception or growth of any tree comment sapling, shrub, underwood, gorse, or other plant.

   Where the Council prohibit the use by any such wheeled chair, perambulator, or chaise of any such part of the stray as may be fixed by the Council and may be described in a noticeboard affixed or set up in some conspicuous position in the stray, a person shall not wheel or station any such chair, perambulator, or chaise, or cause, or suffer any such chair, perambulator, or chaise to be wheeled or stationed over or upon such part of the stray.

11. A person, other than an officer of the council, or a person acting in pursuance of their directions in that behalf, shall not affix or post any bill, placard, or notice to or upon any wall or fence in or enclosing the stray, or to or upon any tree, or other plant, or two or upon any part of any building, barrier, or railing, or of any fixed or moveable seat, or of any other structure or erection in the stray.

12. A person shall not at any time remove or disturb any part of the soil of any flower bed, or any other soil in any part of the stray.

13. A person shall not at any time, in any part of the stray, walk, run, stand, sit, or lie upon any flower bed, shrub, or plant, or any ground in course of preparation as a flower bed, or for the growth of any tree, shrub, or plant.

14. A person shall not at any time, in any part of the stray remove, cut or displace any soil, turf, or plant.

15. A person shall not at any time, in any part of the stray, pluck any bud, blossom, flower, or leaf of any tree, shrub, or plant.

16. A person shall not wilfully, carelessly, or negligently soil or defile any part of any wall or fence in or enclosing the stray, or any part of any building, barrier, or railing, or of any fixed or moveable seat, or of any monument, work of art, ornament, or decoration, or of any other structure or erection in the stray, or wilfully, carelessly, or negligently throw or deposit any filth, rubbish, or refuse, or cause or suffer any filth, rubbish, or refused to fall ought to be thrown all deposited upon any part of the stray.

17. A person shall not wilfully, carelessly, or negligently throw or discharge in the stray any stone or other missile to the damage or danger of any person.

18. A person shall not climb any wall or fence in or enclosing the stray, or any tree, or any barrier, railing, post, or other erection in the stray.

19. A person shall not bathe, wade, or wash in any lake, pond, stream, or other ornamental water in the stray, or wilfully, carelessly, or negligently foul or pollute any such water, or take, injure, or destroy, or attempt to take, injure, or destroy, or wilfully disturb any fish in any such water, or wilfully disturb or worry or ill treat any foul in any such water, or elsewhere in the stray.

20. A person shall not, in any part of the stray, wilfully displace or disturb, injure, or destroy any bird's nest, or wilfully take, injure, or destroy any bird's egg.

21. A person shall not, in any part of the stray, take, injure, or destroy any bird, or spread or use any net, or set or use any snare or other engine, instrument, or means for the taking, injury, or destruction of any bird.

22. A person shall not cause or suffer any dog belonging to him or in his charge to enter or remain in the stray, unless such dog be and continue to be effectually restrained from causing annoyance to any person, and from worrying or disturbing any beast, and from injuring or destroying, worrying or disturbing any fowl in the stray.

23. A person shall not solicit any gift or subscription or make any collection in the stray, except with the consent in writing of the Council.

   Provided that nothing in this byelaw shall interfere with the operation of any regulation made under Sec. 5 of the Police, Factories, etc. (Miscellaneous Provisions), Act, 1916, for the time being in force in the Urban District of Hipperholme.

24. A person shall not deliver or read any public speech, lecture, prayer, sermon or address of any kind, or sing any sacred or secular song, or enter into any public discussion, or hold or take part in any public assemblage in the stray without the consent, in writing, of the council.

25. A person shall not play or make sounds on any musical instrument in the stray without the consent, in writing, of the council.

26. Where the council set apart any such part of the stray as may be fixed by the council, and may be described in a noticeboard affixed or set up in some conspicuous position in the stray, for the purpose of any game specified in the notice board, which, by reason of the rules or manner of playing, or for the prevention of damage, danger, or discomfort to any person in the stray, may necessitate, at any time during the continuance of the game, the exclusive use by the player or players of any part of the stray:-

   A person a person shall not and any space elsewhere in this tray play or take part in any game so specified in such a manner as to exclude persons not playing or taking part in the game from the use of such space.

27. Every person resorting to the stray for the purpose of playing or taking part in any game which by reason of the rules or manner of playing, or for the prevention of damage, danger, or discomfort to any person in the stray, may necessitate, at any time during the continuance of the game, the exclusive use of any space in the stray, shall comply with the following requirements:-

   (1.) He shall, in making preparation for the playing of such game and in the manner of playing, used reasonable and proper care to prevent undue interference with the reasonable and proper use of the stray by other persons:

   (2.) He shall not at any time in any part of a space which is already occupied by other players begin to play without the permission of such other players:

   (3.) Except in any case where the exclusive use of any space may have been granted by the Council for the playing of any match, of which the occasion and character shall be such as to render expedient an extension of the time hereinafter specified, a player or company of players shall not, in in making preparation for playing and in playing any game, use any part of such space for a longer time than *two hours* continuously, if at the expiration of that time any other player or company of players, for whose use no other part of the stray may be available, shall make known to such first-mentioned player or company of players an intention to use, for the purpose of playing, such space as shall have been previously used by such player or company of players.

28. A person shall not in any part of the stray which may have been set apart by the Council for any game play or take part in any such game at any time when on account of the wetness of the ground or of any other cause such part is unfit for use and a notice is affixed or set up in some conspicuous position in the stray prohibiting play in such part.

29. A person shall not, except as hereinafter provided, erect any post, rail, fence, pole, tent, booth, stand, building, or other structure in any part of the stray:

Provided that the foregoing prohibition shall not apply in any case where, upon an application to the council for permission to erect any post, rail, fence, pole, tent, booth, stand, building, or other structure in any part of the stray, upon such occasion and for such purpose as shall be specified in such application, the council may grant permission to any person to erect such post, rail, fence, pole, tent, booth, stand, building, or other structure.

30. A person shall not, in any part of the stray, beat, shake, sweep, brush, or cleanse any carpet, drugget, rug, or mat, or any other fabric retaining dust or dirt.

31. A person shall not, in any part of the stray, hang, spread, or deposit any linen or other fabric for the purpose of drying or bleaching.

32. A person shall not, in any part of the stray, sell, or offer or expose for sale, or let to hire, or offer or expose for letting to hire, any commodity or article, unless, in pursuance of an agreement with the Council, or otherwise in the exercise of any lawful right or privilege, search person may be duly authorised to sell or let to hire in the stray such commodity or article.

33. A person shall not, in any part of the stray, wilfully obstruct, disturb, interrupt, or annoy any other person in the proper use of the stray, or wilfully obstruct, disturb, or interrupt any officer of the Council in the proper execution of his duty, or any person or servant of any person employed by the Council in the proper execution of any work in connexion with the laying out, planting, improvement, or maintenance of the stray.

34. A person shall not in the stray use any indecent or obscene language to the annoyance of any person.

35. Every person who shall offend against any of the foregoing byelaws shall be liable for every such offence to a penalty of *five pounds*:

Provided, nevertheless, that the justices or caught before whom any complaint may be made or any proceedings may be taken in respect of any such offence may, if they think fit, a judge the payment, as a penalty of any sum less than the full amount of the penalty imposed by this byelaw.

36. Every person who shall infringe any byelaw for the regulation of the stray may be removed there from by any officer of the Council, or by any constable, in any one of the several cases hereinafter specified; that is to say, —

(i.)   where the infraction of the byelaw is committed within the view of such officer or constable, and the name and residence of the person infringing the bylaw are unknown to and cannot be readily ascertained by such officer or constable:

(ii.)   where the infraction of the bylaw is committed within the view of such officer or constable, and, from the nature of such infraction, or from any other fact of which such officer or constable may have knowledge, or of which he may be credibly informed, there may be reasonable ground for belief that the continuance in the stray of the person infringing the byelaw may result another infraction of a byelaw, or that the removal of such person from the stray is otherwise necessary as a security for the proper use and regulation thereof.

Given under the Common Seal of the said Urban District Council of Hipperholme this

day of   1925

Chairman

SEAL

Clerk

Allowed by the Minister of Health this

day of   1925.

SEAL

Assistant Secretary, Ministry of Health.

Sources

Barker, D. & Philp, I, *In the Shadow of Lightcliffe's Old Tower: Two Churches and a Churchyard* (Lightcliffe, 2022).

Brooke, J. M., *Educating the Generations* (Lightcliffe, 2020).

Greenwood, A., *Drawn on the Landscape* (Lightcliffe, 2023).

Horne, R. M. & Brooke, J. M., (compiled and edited), *Village Voices* (2007).

Horsfall Turner, J. *The History of Brighouse, Rastrick and Hipperholme* (1893); reprint published by MTD Rigg (Publications), (Leeds, 1983).

Mitchell, G. *LGC Centenary, 1907-2007* (Privately published, 1907).

Parker, J. *Illustrated Rambles from Hipperholme to Tong,* (Bradford 1903).

Thomas, P., *Seeing It Through: Halifax & Calderdale During World War II*, (Hebden Bridge, 2005).

Minutes of Hipperholme Urban District Council (1918-37), Brighouse Council (1937-74), Calderdale Metropolitan District Council (1974-77).

Brighouse Echo / Brighouse & Elland Echo
Brighouse News
Halifax Evening Courier

Lightcliffe & District Local History Society – www.lightcliffehistory.org
Malcolm Bull's *Calderdale Companion* – www.calderdalecompanion.co.uk
Wikipedia – www.wikipedia.org
www.ancestry.co.uk
www.findmypast.co.uk

NOTES

Chapter 1   Some History

[1] Extensive details of the life and career of Samuel Washington are available in two splendidly detailed and literate works of research and reference: the website of The Friends of St. Matthew's Churchyard (https://www.lightcliffechurchyard.org.uk), and D. Barker & I. Philp, *In the Shadow of Lightcliffe's Old Tower: Two Churches and a Churchyard* (Lightcliffe, 2022).

[2] George Hepworth (1799-1875) was a Brighouse architect and surveyor. J. Horsfall Turner, in *The History of Brighouse, Rastrick and Hipperholme* (first published 1893, reprinted 1985 by MTD Rigg) writes that the Hepworth family 'have been located at Yew Trees and Hove Edge for centuries. One of his sons, also George Hepworth (1849-1929), was a Brighouse architect and artist, working in the practice Hepworth & Son set up by his father. The son was a keen photographer, founder of the Brighouse Photographic Society in 1894. His 1885 publication *Brighouse: Its Scenery and Antiquities*, dedicated to John Lister of Shibden Hall, *'To Whom The History And Antiquities Of Many Places Described In The Following Pages Are Of Special Interest'*, is one of the earliest photographic records of our area.

[3] See https://www.chrishelme-brighouse.org.uk for a wealth of local material, including details of Chris's many publications. He also gives talks on a number of other subjects, often to audiences of holidaymakers cruising around Northern Europe and the Mediterranean.

[4] J. Parker, *Illustrated Rambles from Hipperholme to Tong*, (Bradford, 1904), p.475.

[5] *Echo*, 17 March 1988.

[6] https://smithson.org.uk/2002/03/smithson-notes-and-memoirs/ This website contains a detailed history of the Smithson family. They were wealthy but it doesn't seem likely that any member of the family could have left large sums of money to Joshua and Joseph in the early 1870s.

[7] I first became aware of this through the deeds to Netherfield, Wakefield Road, Lightcliffe, and Lynton, Sutherland Road. Thanks to Philip and Sarah Iredale, and Francis and Stoker.

[8] Charles and 'J' Smithson played cricket for Lightcliffe in the 1880s and into the 1890s. There is no way of knowing whether 'J' was Joshua or Joseph, although in 1880, when J. Smithson first appears in the team, Joshua was eighteen, his brother Joseph thirteen, so it seems most likely it was the former. In 1881, when his younger brothers were boarding at the Quaker school at Ackworth, Joshua was an 'Apprentice Stuff Printer', presumably in the family business. Charles and 'J' were also prominent members of the Friends' schoolroom at Slead Syke. On one occasion, the *Brighouse News* of 17 March 1888 informs us, Charles gave a lecture on The Lake District to the Friends, showing sixty photos with an 'oxy-hydrogen lantern, manipulated by J. Smithson'. Frustratingly, 'J', again, is not identified. As an irrelevant but, I hope, interesting aside, the newspaper records that a large party, including the Smithsons, had taken a house in Ambleside at £3.12s. for the week. There were photographing tours to Windermere, Rydal, Coniston, Grasmere, and the Langdale Pikes. At the end of the week the members of the party found that 'their expenses per head, excluding rail fare, were £1-14s.'
[9] *Echo*, 14 September 1923.

[10] At the opening ceremony, Brighouse millowner Thomas Ormerod 'congratulated the Liberals of Hipperholme on their club. Up to the year 1872, they had regarded Hipperholme as a forcing ground

of Toryism but the superior gentility of the people of Hipperholme (laughter) altered those matters now'. (*Brighouse News*, 17 December 1881.)

[11] During those five-and-a-quarter hours 2,738 men, from both sides, were killed. Just because people who were not directly involved in fighting liked the symmetry of 11/11/11. This single act symbolises the callousness and selfishness of most political and military leaders throughout history.

[12] Herbert Lancaster Taylor (1878-1953) was born in Trawden, Lancashire. He became vicar of St. Matthew's, Lightcliffe, in 1914, having been a curate at Mirfield and vicar of Scisset. He was canonised in the 1930s.

[13] Goldthorp, Colonel Robert Howard (1881-1955). During World War I, he served with the 4th West Riding Regiment, (T.F.), attached to 2nd-10th London Regiment, Lightcliffe. He was a director of Firths' Carpets for forty years until his death. Goldthorp and his family lived at Holroyd House, Priestley Green from the end of World War I, after the closure of Priestley Green Hospital.

[14] George Hague was headmaster from 1906-24, Ethel Womersley a teacher from 1902 to 1947, an amazing forty-five years. For more information, see John Brooke, *Educating the Generations*, (Lightcliffe 2020).

[15] The cricket ground was at Upper Rookes Farm, between what is now the Calderdale Way and Rookes Lane. In 1919 Norwood Green Cricket Club played in the Halifax Parish League. (They were league champions in 1921.) The club folded shortly at the beginning of the Second World War, after which it was used by Craven Gentlemen C.C. Later it was the home of Wyke C.C, an amalgamation of three Wyke teams: Wyke Temperance, Wyke Westfield, and Lower Wyke Moravians. By the millennium a new Norwood Green team played at the ground, but they too have perished. It is now pasture land.

[16] Southowram Prize Band was formed in 1901. In 1923 they won a special prize for cornet playing at Crystal Palace. They folded in 1938.

[17] R. Bretton, *Hipperholme & Lightcliffe*, Halifax Antiquarian Society Transaction No. 526, October 1957.

[18] Newton Brooke (1856-1935) was the fifth child and middle son of Joseph Brooke, who started the local quarrying business in 1940. This became Joseph Brooke Ltd., then Joseph Brooke & Sons Ltd. Newton was chairman of the company from 1903, succeeding his brother, Willie, who had died in a railway accident near his Park Terrace home. Newton was also a Hipperholme councillor, chairman of the Council, and an alderman. In March 1890 he was sued for breach of promise by Hannah Haley of Northowram. She was awarded £700 damages. In 1897 Brooke married Edith Sutcliffe. The family lived at Fernside, and The Grange, Lightcliffe.

[19] William Carver Womersley (1857-1922) had a printing business in Halifax. He lived at 2, Cresswell Terrace, Lightcliffe. William was a Hipperholme councillor, chairman of the Council, and chairman of Lightcliffe Cricket Club, an organisation of which he was an influential member for many years. His son, William Dobson Womersley, was Professor of Engineering at Peterhouse College, Cambridge. He tutored Christopher Cockrell, the inventor of the hovercraft.

[20] *Echo*, 9 May 1919.

[21] Whitley, Brigadier-General Sir Edward Nathan (1873-1966). Half-brother of J. H. Whitley (who conducted the opening ceremony of the Stray, as will be seen), he was educated at Clifton College, Bristol, and Trinity College, Cambridge, after which he entered the legal profession. Among the many posts he held were honorary secretary of the Halifax Literary & Philosophical Society and president of the Halifax Building Society (1938-1945). Whitley was an officer in the 2nd West Riding Yorkshire Volunteer Artillery (1896-1917). During World War I he attained the rank of Brigadier General, taking a battalion of the Royal Field Artillery from Halifax to France. He was mentioned in despatches. He was knighted on 4 June 1921. Whitley was buried in the family grave at Lister Lane Cemetery (Plot Number 456).

[22] Rev. Horrox had arrived at Lightcliffe Congregational church in 1917, succeeding Rev. W.D. ffrench. He was to remain as minister until 1957.

[23] *Echo*, 6 June 1919.

[24] *Echo*, 30 May 1919.

[25] *Echo*, 6 June 1919.

[26] Col. Richard Edgar Sugden (1871-1951) was the grandson of Thomas Sugden, who started the Brighouse flour milling business in about 1835. (See also p.98.) He was captain of the Brighouse Rangers rugby team and played for Yorkshire in 1895 and 96. Sugden saw service with the Imperial Yeomanry in the Boer War, and in 1904 joined the 4th Battalion, Duke of Wellingtons Regiment. In 1907 he married Alice Healey, who tragically died following a skating accident while on honeymoon in Paris. In 1910 he married Nora. They lived at Newlands, off Huddersfield Road. Sugden was wounded at Ypres in the First World War, and was later awarded the D.S.O. and bar. President of the Brighouse Chamber of Trade, he was made a Freeman of the Borough in 1943.

[27] I have only read of this view being expressed by those in command; never a member of the rank and file.

[28] Thomas Wardingley, the bugler, was my great grandfather. He and his three sons, Harold, Admiral (my grandfather), and George, were in France for much of the war. While they were away, Thomas's wife, Ellen, died. Family tradition has the cause as being a broken heart. The 1901 census returns contain only the names of Ellen and her three sons. Thomas was away at the Boer War.

[29] *Echo*, 6 June 1919.

[30] Sir William Henry Aykroyd (1865-1947) was created the first Baronet of Lightcliffe in the king's birthday honours of 1920. The following year he became chairman of T. F. Firth & Sons, in succession to his uncle, Sir Algernon Firth. William had married Emma Hammond, of the Bradford brewing business, in 1890. He became managing director of that company, as well as managing director of the Bradford Dyers Association. The Aykrods, who lived at Cliffe Hill, gave the land and the war memorial to Bailiff Bridge. William was also president of Lightcliffe Cricket Club. In 1922 he paid for a new pavilion, which lasted for 101 years.

[31] The architect Joseph Frederick Walsh (1861-1950) was born at Thornhill, Hipperholme, the youngest of nine children. In 1877, he was articled to his uncle Richard Horsfall. During a long career he was a member of several partnerships, that with George Maddock (1878-1939) being of longest duration. Maddock was also a governor of the Royal Halifax Infirmary. Their work included The

Beehive and Cross Keys, The Commercial at Illingworth, Ebenezer Primitive Methodist Chapel, The Friendly at Boothtown, and St. John the Divine, Rishworth. Locally, Walsh designed George Street, Craig Royston on Bramley Lane, the old Lightcliffe vicarage behind the church, and the headmaster's house and boys' dormitories at Hipperholme Grammar School. Walsh was a Lightcliffe cricketer.

Edward Caldwell Spruce (1865-1922) was born in Knutsford, Cheshire. Between 1891 and 1893 he was a student at the Leeds College of Art where he also taught clay modelling. Spruce first worked at a local tile factory before moving to Burmantofts Pottery in Leeds, where he was principal modeller. His work there includes some fine panels on the Midland Hotel, Manchester. He went to Paris to study art and returned to Leeds to set up as a freelance artist with a studio in Chapeltown, Leeds.

[32] Sir Brigadier-General George Ayscough Armytage (1872-1953) was 7th Baronet of Kirklees. He served with the King's Royal Rifle Corps during World War I and became Brigadier-General in 1916. He was appointed C.M.G., awarded the D.S.O. and the Croix de Guerre. An amateur archaeologist, he excavated and revealed the foundations of the main buildings of Kirklees Priory in 1902.

[33] Field Marshall Sir William Robert Robertson, 1st Baronet (1860-1933) was a British Army officer who served as Chief of the Imperial General Staff – the professional head of the British Army – from 1916 to 1918. In November 1877 he had enlisted as a trooper in the 16th (The Queen's) Lancers. He was 17 years old, but declared his age to be eighteen years and two months. During the First World War he was committed to a Western Front strategy focusing on Germany and was against what he saw as peripheral operations on other fronts. Robertson had increasingly poor relations with David Lloyd George, Secretary of State for War and then Prime Minister, and threatened resignation at Lloyd George's attempt to subordinate the British forces to the French Commander-in-Chief, Robert Nivelle. In 1917 Robertson supported the continuation of the Battle of Passchendaele (also known as the Third Battle of Ypres) at odds with Lloyd George's view that Britain's war effort ought to be focused on the other theatres until the arrival of sufficient U.S. troops on the Western Front.

[34] Harold Hammond Aykroyd (1896-1974) was the second son of Emma and William Henry. Second-Lieutenant Aykroyd had served with the 1st/4th Battalion Duke of Wellington's (West Riding Regiment). He was awarded the Military Cross in 1916. He and his older brother, Alfred, were chairmen of T. F. Firth & Sons Ltd., Harold succeeding Alfred in 1962. Alfred had become the 2nd Baronet of Lightcliffe on the death of their father in 1947. Both played cricket for Lightcliffe. Harold was an accomplished batsman.

[35] Captain Maynard Percy Andrews (1871-1915) was appointed headmaster of Hipperholme Grammar School in 1911 and in the same year joined the 1/4th Battalion Duke of Wellington's Regiment (West Riding) in Halifax. He was quickly promoted to lieutenant and then to captain in October 1914. Andrews was deployed to France on April 14, 1915, as second-in-command of A Company and was followed into battle by former, and then current, pupils of the school. While in Command of A Company he was killed in Flanders on Saturday, August 14 1915 while trying to bring his wounded men to safety. Andrews was described by a commanding officer as "one of the straightest, cleanest, and healthiest-minded men I have ever met."

[36] John Lister (1847-1933) was the last Lister of Shibden Hall. In a lifetime of many accomplishments, he was a founder member of the Independent Labour Party and a founder and the first president of Halifax Antiquarian Society. He was chairman of the Governors of Hipperholme Grammar School

for twenty-five years until his death. He wrote the school song, in Latin. Sing, or even recite, the first line – *Seu labore dolet testa* – to an old boy of a certain vintage, and he will enthusiastically take up the refrain. The theme of the song is that schooldays are the best days of your life, and that the friendships and memories of those times should never be allowed to fade away. Hmmm.

[37] *Echo*, 27 June 1919.

[38] *Echo*, 23 September 1921.

[39] Some details of the life of Harry Percy Jackson (1867-1931) can be found through the following link – https://www.lightcliffehistory.org.uk/topics/38-jackson-of-coley. Jackson's house and workshop were at Morriscot on Coley Road, next to the Sunday school.

[40] The origin of this phrase is unclear, but certainly predates the First World War. Indeed, it may have its genesis as long ago as Ancient Greece, when a variant was used by philosopher and historian Plutarch.

Chapter 3   Deliberation

[41] *Echo*, 9 August 1919.

[42] *Echo*, 5 September 1919.

[43] The sloping field at the commencement of the proposed footpath crosses land which was in the ownership of Lightcliffe Golf Club (founded 1907). Then, as now, the third green and fourth tee occupied part of this area north of Helliwell Syke. As the route of the proposed path refers to 'the footpath from the road to the stream' I take it that it was to follow the public right of way which existed then, as it does now. Strange that there is no mention of the golf club's ownership, especially as this section was to have 'steps at intervals in an avenue of trees'. The proposal also refers to a 'golf green' on the south side of the viaduct. The earliest version of the course had three holes on the south-east side of the railway line. (Information from *Lightcliffe Golf Club Centenary 1907-2007*, by Grayham Mitchell.)

Chapter 4   Decision

[44] As is evident from the letterhead, clerk to Hipperholme Urban District Council was a part-time appointment. Francis Marriner Horner (1878-1950) was the son of Charles Horner and his first wife, Sarah. In the 1850s Charles started a jewellery and watch-making business in Hebden Bridge, moving to Northgate, Halifax, in the 1870s. He is best known now as the inventor of the 'Dorcas' thimble, improving the conventional soft silver thimble by using alternating layers of steel to strengthen the product. Charles and his family lived from 1875 until his death in 1896 at what is now The Poplars, next to the junction of St. Giles Road with Wakefield Road, appropriately opposite the south-east corner of Smithson Park, the fields which would become the Stray. Francis would have spent his early years near to the house and lands of Joshua Smithson.

[45] *Echo*, 3 November 1922.

[46] *Echo*, 10 November 1922.

[47] Rowland Lumb lived at Longlands, Leeds & Whitehall Road.

[48] Herbert Womersley (1880-1958) was the sixth of the ten children of Crossley and Rose (née Swales) Womersley. In 1891 they kept the White Horse Inn on Leeds Road. Crossley died in 1895. Rose stayed at the White Horse. In 1901 and 1911 she was the landlady, assisted by adult children. Herbert was a Hipperholme councillor for many years, subsequently a member of the Brighouse Council, and was mayor of Brighouse from 1940-42. He was a partner in the Hipperholme machine tool firm of Womersley and Broadbent. One of his sisters, Ethel Womersley, mentioned elsewhere in the book, was a teacher at Lightcliffe school.

[49] Thomas Holgate (1865-1948) was born in Methley, but by the time he was six, according to the census return of 1871, the family lived at 'Hill Top, Lidget", his father a 'Farm Bailiffe'. They were later at Hoyle House, where the sixteen-year-old Thomas is described as 'Farmer's Son'. In 1891 he married Annie Hobson. They lived on Ripley Street at first, and in the census of that year Thomas is a 'Farmer's Labourer'. However, ten years later they have moved to Till Carr Farm and he is described as 'Farmer. Employer.' They stayed at the farm until, sometime perhaps in the early 1920s, they moved to 1, Syke Terrace, by which time he must have been semi-retired, although he still kept some cows in the small field next to his house, where the White Horse car park is now situated. As we have seen he grazed these cows on Smithson Park, before it became the Stray. Thomas Holgate was a Hipperholme councillor for thirty years, and the final chairman of the Council in 1936-7, before the Brighouse takeover.

[50] *Echo*, 1 December 1922.

[51] For E. B. Osborn see following note.

[52] Bernard Osborn(e), whose name sometimes appears with the concluding 'e', lived at Lydgate House. He was there from about 1920 until 1947. In the 1911 census return, when he lived at Knowl House, he spelt his surname 'Osborne'. He was the brother of Ernest Bacon Osborn, whose name almost always lacks the 'e', the one exception being the list of donors to the Stray Memorial Fund. Ernest lived at Lightcliffe House, next to Smith House, on the site of the present Windsor Walk. There is a mystery surrounding the naming of Osborne Grove, the terrace above Westfield, off Wakefield Road, built in 1905. (Thanks to Merlin Kalanovic for this information.) It would seem probable that there was a connection with the Osborne family, although I have never seen confirmation of this.

Charles Rose was at Rylstone, 53, Wakefield Road, the house next to the Stray as you enter from Wakefield Road just above Lightcliffe Club.

Walter Naylor lived at Lydgate House in 1911, although he died in December of that year. The *Echo* report of the opening specifies 'the executors of the late Mr. Naylor'. Lot 7, Lydgate House, didn't sell in the 1907 auction. Perhaps Mr. Naylor purchased the premises shortly afterwards.

The only Baines I have been able to trace is James Arthur Baines, who lived at 17, Wakefield Road at the time of the 1924 Electoral register, well removed from the Stray boundary. In his concluding remarks Francis Horner, clerk to the Council, remarks how they were 'indebted to Mr. B. O. Osborn, Mr. Rose and Mr Naylor for the way in which they had met the committee with regard to portions of the land.' No reference to the Baines family.

[53] Edward John Reddie lived at 12, The Crescent.

Fred Pohlmann was at Oakleigh, Brighouse Road, the detached house at the southern end of Waverley Terrace. His occupation in the 1901 and 1911 census returns is 'Pianoforte Manufacturer'. He is an

'Employer' with a business in Halifax. Some will remember Pohlmann's on Cornmarket. The photograph below is dated 1978.

(Dave Lister Collection)

[54] *Echo*, 16 February 1923.

[55] The verb 'to twit', meaning to 'tease or taunt, especially in a good-humoured way' has become archaic, but it is interesting that, a mere hundred years ago, it was acceptable, if not common, usage.

[56] This ironic phrase is from Vernon Scannell's poem 'The Great War', published in his 1962 collection, *A Sense of Danger*.

Chapter 5   Opening Ceremony

[57] The Right Honourable John Henry Whitley, P.C. was the half-brother of Sir Edward Nathan Whitley (see Note 21 above). Educated at Clifton College and London University, he then worked in the family cotton-spinning business on Hanson Lane, Halifax. In 1893 he became a Halifax town councillor, and in 1900 he entered parliament as Liberal M.P. for Halifax (1900-18). He was subsequently Speaker of the House of Commons (1921-28). In 1930 he was appointed chairman of the B.B.C. J.H. Whitley School was named after him. He is buried in Lister Lane Cemetery.

[58] Rev. Tomsen lived at 16, Westfield. Later, by the 1950s, Lightcliffe curates lived at 11, Westfield.

[59] This is the final line of Philip Larkin's poem MCMXIV, from his collection *Whitsun Weddings*, published by Faber & Faber in 1964.

[60] Again, thanks to Chris Helme for a copy of this letter.

[61] The whist drive raised £60.10s.0d., as reported to the committee in February.

Chapter 6   The Early Years – 1924-39

[62] These were representatives of Louis John Bancroft of Craigmore, Holly Bank, Lillian Annie Hind of Elm Grange, and James Sykes of Oak House. This is the James Sykes who helped to develop the gardens around the memorial.

[63] As I said in the introduction, I do not intend to provide a long list of references to meetings. If anyone wishes to follow up any of the points I make, it is obvious enough when the meetings took place. Calderdale Libraries have copies of the Hipperholme U.D.C. minutes.

[64] The *Brighouse Echo* was the *Brighouse and Elland Echo* from 1923-51, after which it reverted to its original title.

[65] George Walsh (1847-1929) was the second of John and Anne Walsh's nine children, Joseph the last. George was a stuff merchant's agent. In 1891 he and Joseph were the only two still living with their mother, on Cobden Terrace. Their father had died in 1870, aged fifty-seven. George later lived with his sister Mary Ann, the eighth child.

[66] This is from the deeds of Netherfield. Thanks again to the Iredales. It is similar to the plan in the Lynton deeds, part of which has been reproduced on p. 4, except that it shows that the plot on which Lynton was built has already been sold. (This is the square alongside Sutherland Road.)

[67] Philip C. Tordoff, as head of music at Hipperholme Grammar School for forty years from 1962, was at one time my teacher, later a colleague. Among his many and diverse interests is historical gas lamps.

[68] Dorron Harper has a Halifax lantern and gas burner in his collection. He says that when Brighouse superseded Hipperholme U.D.C. in 1937, the gas would have still been bought from Halifax. However, after nationalisation in 1949, the North Eastern Gas Board took over. Dorron asks the question, "Who maintained the gas lamps then?" Halifax was possibly unique (Dorron informs me) in being the only local authority which manufactured its own gas lamps, and obviously sold some to other authorities. These were phased out during the 1960s and early 1970s. At one time there had been more than 3,000 gas lamps in the Halifax area; by 1970, there were about 50. Dorron services the lamps of the Keighley and Worth Valley Railway.

[69] *Echo*, 19 June 1925.

[70] Grayham Mitchell, *Lightcliffe Golf Club Centenary 1907-2007*. Privately printed and distributed.

[71] John Millington was a founder member of the Lightcliffe & District Local History Society. Brought up on Mountfields, Bramley Lane, he has a thorough memory of his early years in the village and has spoken many times to the society on the Hipperholme and Lightcliffe of his childhood.

[72] *Echo*, 19 June 1925.

[73] Advert in *The Brodleian*, termly magazine of Hipperholme Grammar School, for December 1935.

[74] Russell, D., *Popular Music in England, 1840-1914*, second edition (Manchester, 1997), p.205.

[75] Ibid., p.215. (Dave Russell lived on Osborne Grove, Lightcliffe, in the 1980s and 90s.)

[76] Ibid., p.215.

Presumably, this was regarded as not being worthwhile. In 1926, the Council had received only £2.7s.7d. from the summer's concerts.

Chapter 7   World War Two

[78] 'This is a war to end all wars' is a phrase from an article written by H. G. Wells in the *Daily News* of 14 August 1914, entitled 'The War That Will End War'.

[79] I had never heard of this ironic pseudonym, and am grateful to local man Derryck Milligan for the information.

[80] The Service of Youth Council may have been a precursor to the British Youth Council, which was founded in 1948.

[81] 7 January 1998. See Horne & Brooke, *Village Voices* (Lightcliffe, 2007), p.4.

Chapter 8   Never Had It So Good

[82] There is a Wicksteed Park in Kettering, a Grade II English Heritage Listed Park and Garden.

[83] 'Mischief Night is an informal holiday on which children, teenagers and adults engage in jokes, pranks, vandalism, or parties. It is known by a variety of names including Devil's Night, Gate Night, Goosey Night, Moving Night, Cabbage Night, Mystery Night and Mat Night.' For further information on this 230-year-old tradition, see https://en.wikipedia.org/wiki/Mischief_Night, from which the above quotation is taken.

[84] Ken Pickard, a pupil at Hipperholme Grammar School in the 1930s, was a Hipperholme resident all his life. A teacher and local historian, it was Ken who came up with the idea of naming the new secondary school, built in the late 1960s on Stoney Lane, Lightcliffe, 'Eastfield', in recognition of the status of that area in the ancient township of Hipperholme.

[85] Rev. Lewis was curate at St. Matthew's, Lightcliffe, from 1955 to 1957, when he became vicar of Bradshaw.

[86] 11, Westfield was either owned or rented on a long-term basis by St. Matthew's church. I was brought up on Park Terrace and lived almost directly opposite the 'curate house'. Rev. Lewis is the first I remember. He was followed by Ian Knox, who went to St. Matthew's, Rastrick, and Brian Abell.

[87] I cannot find the source of this quotation, which I came across while trying to source another snow quotation – the poem which contains the line, 'Snow covers the earth in forgetful silence'. I couldn't find that one either.

[88] A drumhead service is a traditional army service held in the field, in which regimental drums are placed on top of each other to form an altar.

Index

Lightcliffe & District Local History Society

The society is now in its twenty-seventh year. For details log into *www.lightcliffehistory.org.uk*. During this time audiences have enjoyed well over a hundred talks on the history of our area. Below is a small sample of titles.

The Rise and Fall of Crow Nest.

St. Matthew's Church Registers.

Anne Lister of Shibden Hall.

Crime and Punishment in Hipperholme and Lightcliffe.

The History of Coley Hall.

Pavilions of Splendour – the first 50 years of Lightcliffe Cricket Club.

Lightcliffe School Log Books.

Postcards from Lightcliffe – early postcards of the village.

Local Buildings and Workers' Housing.

Jackson of Coley – the work of the woodcarver Harry Percy Jackson.

The Walkers of Lightcliffe – Ann Walker and her family.

Hipperholme Urban District Council, 1894-1937.

Rhubarb, Rhubarb – the story of the Priestley Green market gardens.

Highways and Byways – the ancient routes between Halifax and Lightcliffe.

The Moravians Came to Smith House.

St. Matthew's Old Church Revisited.

Walterclough – the recent history of Red Beck valley.